PAM ALLYN & ERNEST MORRELL

FOREWORD BY MARIAN WRIGHT EDELMAN

EVERY CHILD A SUPER READER

2ND EDITION

7 Strengths for a Lifetime of
Independence, Purpose, and Joy

SCHOLASTIC

For Jeannie, friend of my heart.
I thank you for the pond of us,
the shining, glistening, clear waters
of a friendship that perseveres, persists,
continues, stays steady on its course.

—P. A.

To my three super readers, Amani,
Antonio, and Tripp Morrell.
—E. M.

Credits

Cover Design: Tannaz Fassihi
Interior Design: Maria Lilja
Interior photographs and video: Monet Izabeth Eliastam
Acquiring Editor: Lois Bridges
Development Editor: Raymond Coutu
Editorial Director: Sarah Longhi
Senior Editor: Shelley Griffin
Production Editor: Danny Miller

Photos ©: 27: FatCamera/Getty Images; 163: FatCamera/Getty Images. All other photos ©: Monet Izabeth Eliastam.

Pages 50–51: From *All Because You Matter*. Text copyright © 2020 by Tami Charles. Illustrations copyright © 2020 by Bryan Collier. Used by permission of Scholastic Inc.; 64–65: From *Maybe Tomorrow?* Text copyright © 2019 by Charlotte Agell. Illustrations copyright © 2019 by Ana Ramírez González. Used by permission of Scholastic Inc.; 76–77: From *Addy's Cup of Sugar*. Text and illustrations copyright © 2020 by Jon J Muth. Used by permission of Scholastic Inc.; 90–91: From *The Magician's Hat*. Text copyright © 2018 by Malcolm Mitchell. Illustrations copyright © 2018 by Joanne Lew-Vriethoff. Used by permission of Scholastic Inc.; 104–105: From *Standing on Her Shoulders*. Text copyright © 2021 by Monica Clark-Robinson. Illustrations copyright © 2021 by Laura Freeman. Used by permission of Scholastic Inc.; 116–117: From *The Rooster Who Would Not Be Quiet!* Text copyright © 2017 by Carmen Agra Deedy. Illustrations copyright © 2017 by Eugene Yelchin. Used by permission of Scholastic Inc.; 128–129: From *Martin Rising: Requiem for a King*. Text copyright © 2018 by Andrea Davis Pinkney. Illustrations copyright © 2018 by Brian Pinkney. Used by permission of Scholastic Inc.
All rights reserved.

CONTENTS

Foreword by Marian Wright Edelman 5

Introduction: A World of Super Readers 7

PART I: THE PATH TO CREATING SUPER READERS: THE 7 STRENGTHS FRAMEWORK 13

CHAPTER 1: Why Super Reading Matters Now More Than Ever 14

CHAPTER 2: The 7 Strengths Framework: Independence, Purpose, and Joy 28

CHAPTER 3: Strength One: Belonging 42

CHAPTER 4: Strength Two: Friendship 56

CHAPTER 5: Strength Three: Kindness 69

CHAPTER 6: Strength Four: Curiosity 82

CHAPTER 7: Strength Five: Confidence 96

CHAPTER 8: Strength Six: Courage 108

CHAPTER 9: Strength Seven: Hope 121

PART II: THE 7 STRENGTHS FRAMEWORK IN ACTION 133

CHAPTER 10: Best Practices for Super Readers 134

CHAPTER 11: Structured Independent Reading: The Super Practice 152

CHAPTER 12: Management Strategies for the Super Reader Classroom 161

CHAPTER 13: Assessment Tools for the Super Reader Classroom 170

CHAPTER 14: Planning Tools for the Super Reader Classroom 187

Concluding Thoughts: Strengths for You 198

7 Strengths Children's Books 200

Professional References Cited 204

Index 207

ACKNOWLEDGMENTS

Abundant gratitude to all the children, teens, teachers, and parents with whom we work, especially the LitWorld community of children and their loving teachers. Much gratitude to Marian Wright Edelman for her foreword and for the work she does that changes the world. We are grateful for the partnership of Scholastic and their faith in this vision and work. To Lois Bridges for starting this journey with us with her shining spirit and vision; Tara Welty, for her generous and extraordinary editorial leadership; Ray Coutu, brilliant editor, who makes it all happen and ignites the work with magic; Sarah Longhi, luminous guide; Shelley Griffin, who provides invaluable editorial work; and Danny Miller, glorious wordsmith of the heart. Thanks to Brian LaRossa, Tannaz Fassihi, and Maria Lilja for their beautiful design. To Cheryl Clark, for understanding and manifesting the 7 Strengths vision with such integrity and care. Thanks to Lisa DiMona, agent extraordinaire, whose wise guidance brought us to now.

Deep appreciation to Billy DiMichele whose fiercely generous support for both of us has brought this book to fruition; and to Rose Else-Mitchell whose leadership has created the essential space for us to write into this new world. In gratitude for Dick Robinson, who championed us to not only envision but to create together a world for every child to become a super reader. His legacy will live on in this book, too.

Pam thanks her communities of love and support. To Sally deGozzaldi for weekly predawn booster calls. To Paige Heimark and Cyrilla Ray for their joyful work and support. With thanks to Paul and Lauren Blum whose for helping us bring this work to the world. Appreciation to Amber Peterson, Debbie Lera, and Pam's teams for their generous grace in the midst of very hard times for children. Greatest gratitude to my life partner, Jim, who makes it all possible as the most super of all husbands. He is the embodiment of courage, integrity, and generosity in every step of this life and work together. Heart-filled thanks to our daughters, Katie and Charlotte, our two original little super readers beyond compare who shine so brightly in how they live in the world with wisdom, strength, accomplishment, and kindness, and Katie's inspiring husband, Aaron. With thanks to Pam's wonderful mother, Anne, and in-laws, Cindy and Lou. This trio is the model for how to be together with us in love always. With thanks for Ernest, the best colleague, friend of heart, mind, soul, and co-creator anyone could ask for.

Ernest thanks his lifelong teaching colleagues Jeff Duncan-Andrade, Wayne Yang, and Newin Orante. He thanks the students he has taught over the past 30 years for the laughter, the tears, the inspiration, and the love in this beautiful struggle. He thanks his childhood teachers and coaches for believing in him, for opening the world of books, and for showing him that, with a bit of hard work and dedication, dreams become flesh. He thanks the doctors and nurses of Beacon Memorial Hospital for making this second edition and every day of life possible. He thanks his grandmother and father who provided love and light in life and provide even more guidance and wisdom from the other side. Ernest thanks his mother for her strength, courage, dignity and good morning bible verse texts that she sends without fail. Ernest also thanks his sons Skip, Antonio, and Tripp for giving him reasons to stay active and for keeping his wallet and refrigerator continually empty. And for making him a proud dad. He thanks his co-author and friend, Pam Allyn, for her endless supplies of dreams, courage, and joy. Finally, Ernest would like to thank Dr. Jodene Morrell, for the ongoing conversations that are children's literacy and cohabiting a world that would make their ancestors proud.

FOREWORD

We at the Children's Defense Fund (CDF) have long believed that reading is an indispensable key to unlocking the door to children's dreams and unlimited potential. Our CDF Freedom Schools® program is grounded in a literature-rich environment and reading curriculum centered on excellent books that reflect a variety of cultures, races, and experiences. For some children, it is the first time they have seen books with characters who look like them. Our goal is to help children fall in love with reading, so much so they respond with comments such as, "I enjoyed learning about my history."; "That [book] really inspired me because he came from a rough neighborhood."; "Freedom Schools taught me when I learn, I can have fun with it. It made me a better reader because I can understand things."; and "I see myself, and the books give me hope."

All children deserve to fall in love with the power of the written word to transport them to new worlds and teach them new ideas, and to experience what writer Pat Mora has called *bookjoy*. Yet too many children miss out on that opportunity. In fact, far too many children cannot read at all. The majority of all children in the United States and nearly three-quarters of our Black and Latino children can't read at grade level. They are being sentenced to social and economic death in our rapidly globalizing world. A 21-year-old student teacher described the connection between an inability to read and entrapment in our nation's dangerous pipeline to prison: "If you can't read by third grade, you don't want anyone to know you can't read, so you act out. When you act out, you get grouped with the other kids who act out. They can't read [either]. Because no one can read and no one discusses that they can't read, they end up becoming part of gangs, and everyone there is there for the same reason."

No child deserves to have the doors to the "world of possible" slammed shut. So I am profoundly grateful for this new book. In *Every Child a Super Reader*, Pam Allyn and

Dr. Ernest Morrell share lessons that will help educators and parents everywhere enable more children to become proficient readers. Their book shows how developing every child's confidence, courage, and hope is vital for learning; showcases the transformational power of literacy in a child's life; describes how to create the kinds of safe and supportive learning environments that exclude no child; promotes equity, opportunity, and the chance for every child to be heard; embraces multicultural children's literature and the power of storytelling as a pathway to academic, social, and civic development; and connects the in-school work of literacy education to homes, families, and out-of-school contexts in order to immerse children in a rich, joyful, literate environment brimming with books and conversation about books 365 days a year.

We *can* create this world for all our children. *Every Child a Super Reader* provides a blueprint for nurturing the engaged and fluent readers we want all of our children to be. In the process, we will transform children's lives and life chances.

—**MARIAN WRIGHT EDELMAN**
President, Children's Defense Fund

A WORLD OF SUPER READERS

The Life-Changing Impact of the 7 Strengths

When we wrote the first edition of this book, the 7 Strengths was a new idea. With our colleagues in the field, we had been working alongside the greatest experts on super reading of all: children and teens themselves. We asked them: "What will make you the most powerful reader, thinker, and learner? What are the conditions you need to make that happen? What exists inside of you and within your families that you always carry?" Together with them, we developed this framework: Belonging, Friendship, Kindness, Curiosity, Confidence, Courage, and Hope.

The children themselves helped us to understand that in order to read well, one has to envision a world in which strengths come first. We never could have imagined what would happen next. The 7 Strengths became the backbone of our work, our programs, lessons, and teaching and learning across age and grade levels, across urban, suburban, and rural school districts. We baked these strengths into the pedagogy and practice of programs, including the renowned summer enrichment program LitCamp, which is used by districts far and wide.

Then, we saw something extraordinary happen. Our students, with a framework that shows them they can be and love themselves, began to learn to read more powerfully than ever before. This framework, beginning with the idea of belonging and ending with the idea of hope, is based on the understanding that we constantly travel in a continuum from self to community to world in our learning. This is true in every area of our growth, but especially as readers. We saw that by following a structured framework of the 7 Strengths, our students were able to navigate the shoals of rocky waters in reading and in life itself. Students were able to easily translate what they read to their lives inside and outside of school. We saw how students using this framework increased their energy, commitment, and resolve to the work of learning to read. It was no longer passive and prescriptive. The strengths became a strategy that students could take ownership of, discuss, and use in any and all circumstances. Approaching literacy learning by way of this framework—Belonging, Friendship, Kindness, Curiosity, Confidence, Courage, and Hope—adds dimension and meaning to the work of learning from the books read and the writing done in response to that reading, to the conversations had, and to the celebrations shared.

Reading is still the foremost way we learn who we are, comfort ourselves in times of hardship, get our information when we need it, communicate well with others, and connect meaningfully to the world. Reading, like breathing, feels effortless when you already have it, but when you don't, it's catastrophic.

The years since we published the first edition of this book have only shown us even more the importance and value of a super reading life. When students were lonely, or isolated, or separated from one another, as happened during the pandemic, the ability to read and write connected them, brought them together, and gave them a sense of joy. A principal's read-aloud, a text message from a teacher, a whole-class read—all of these

things kept our students connected and whole at a time when the world felt fragmented and despairing. For those who could not read, the isolation was even more profound. We cannot underestimate the power of a super reading life. It is what makes us whole, energized, and self-realized.

Reading as a Superpower

We can teach every student how to use reading as a superpower to elevate her mind, spirit, and overall sense of well-being. Reading makes us all more powerful. Whether it helps us seek knowledge or makes us laugh on a tough day, or teaches us to understand history, or enables us to get medical treatment, reading is life-changing and life-affirming.

We can teach every student how to use reading as a superpower to elevate her mind, spirit, and overall sense of well-being. Reading makes us all more powerful.

When we raise and teach a super reader, we are showing her how to decode at the speed of light, to relate deeply to a character, and to finish a book in record time. These are all things super readers do well and do routinely. At the same time, we are teaching our super reader how to use reading to make a friend, to achieve success in a subject area, to become independently able to solve problems, and find solutions to questions of knowledge and skill. We are showing her how to find comfort when times are lonely, to laugh when life feels hard, to cry when we need to lament, and to find ourselves in the pages of a book to build courage.

Reading is not only about what the child does when she reads, but also what reading does for the child.

Reading is about reading widely and voluminously across many media, genres, and experiences. And reading online or print text is not an either/or paradigm. We are all reading in a complex, blended world where reading in every modality and on multiple platforms is natural and expected. We won't be able to predict what surface, platform, or device our students will be reading on in five years, much less ten. But for our teaching and work with our students, that's okay. We are teaching, with the super reader methodology, a more expansive way to think about what reading means to all of us in an ever-changing world. Reading is a mobile, portable, fluid, and flexible idea, and teaching reading shifts as these modalities do. The instruction in this book is all geared to that expansiveness: Reading itself is humankind's greatest innovation, not one device or another, which will change by the minute. Let's keep our eyes on the prize: Super reading is the goal. With these skills in abundance, our students are ready for any and all venues in which reading will be the tool they use to make sense of the world.

Foundational skills, such as phonics skills, phonemic awareness, phonetic capabilities, comprehension, fluency, stamina, and learning academic vocabulary, are crucial to your students' reading process, and they can also be taught within a purposeful context: the "why" of reading. The 7 Strengths Framework helps our students to clarify and really internalize the bigger "why" of reading. We read to find courage. We read to find hope. We read to make a friend. We read to absorb knowledge. We read to become independent. We read to learn a skill. We read to connect to others. These are discussions we can and must have with our students.

The 7 Strengths provide our students with a pathway to Super Reader outcomes and give you, their teacher or administrative leader, a way to guide them there. Super Readers:

- feel a sense of belonging in a community of readers and beyond

- form meaningful friendships around conversation about texts

- learn kindness and empathy building by reading books that demonstrate these features and qualities

- explore areas of their curiosity through reading in all subject areas

- develop confidence to get through the most challenging aspects of reading and in all areas of their lives

- build courage to reach high levels of achievement and delight in their reading experience

- cultivate a mindset of hope that pervades every aspect of their lives, both as readers, even when struggling or facing challenges, and in the larger scope of life, seeing what they read as a way to see the wider world and be part of it

The 7 Strengths vision sets us on a path to a new era—where we come together to help every student achieve independence, purpose, and joy, every one of them. The deficit-oriented labels we have historically given students have long-lasting, detrimental effects. We do not use the term "super reader" lightly, nor casually. With this second edition, we are speaking now from a view of having seen that the 7 Strengths of a super reader in action has been life changing for students of all ages, from early childhood through high school. (Long after they graduate from LitCamp, high schoolers remember how they learned to read with the 7 Strengths and many return to teach the younger children.)

"The 7 Strengths vision sets us on a path to a new era—where we come together to help every student achieve independence, purpose, and joy, every one of them."

When we began this endeavor, we were working across many languages and cultures, and we still are. The diversity of language and culture was baked into the 7 Strengths from the start. They make up the most culturally responsive framework because they begin with the stories, lives, and voices of the people

who use them. The 7 Strengths cross all barriers and are understandable everywhere. They are beautiful and meaningful in every language we have encountered. Students are naturally language curators. They readily love words they can carry with them, the sound and/or look of a sentence and words, and the incredible ways words can comfort and guide. The Super Reader Classroom is more than inclusive: it is an environment of belonging where all stories matter, and the strengths show this.

While it's certainly true that students must learn to orchestrate a complex set of strategic actions that enable comprehension and decoding, it's equally true that learning to read is a social-cultural event. Students become readers when they are immersed in a community of readers, surrounded by rich book talk and animated demonstrations of reading, and provided with rich emotional and life skills support. At the same time that we're helping students acquire the technical skills necessary for proficient reading, we are also working to help students develop the confidence and courage to take the risks needed to propel learning forward. Learning to read, like any human endeavor, requires practice, perseverance, and persistence to push through the challenges to proficiency and beyond proficiency, to lifelong joy and accomplishment.

We are entering an age of participatory education in which everyone's voices should and can matter—including and especially children's. The super reader pedagogy offers a new way to think about all students as readers, one that starts with their strengths, the strengths they bring with them, the stories they carry, the humans they are. You'll close this book understanding:

- The definition, hope, and vision for what a super reader is and can be.
- The benefits of strength-based instruction using the 7 Strengths Framework.
- The indispensable powers of reading and why every student should have them.
- The practical life-skill strategies for helping all students become 365-day super readers.
- The formative assessments that measure strength-based literacy work in action.

In this book, we will help you help your students recognize the 7 Strengths within themselves, teaching them the skills they need to build on this framework to become stronger and more confident readers who believe that they can and will succeed.

Starting the Journey

Every Child a Super Reader gives you all the information you need to help you build a Super Reader Classroom—and all the tools you need to implement the model. Chapter 1 explores the benefits of super reading and principles that undergird the development of super readers. Chapter 2 explains the 7 Strengths Framework and the power it holds to create super readers. Chapters 3 through 9 provide in-depth discussions of each strength, as well as strength-specific lessons. And, finally, Chapters 10 through 14 provide what you need to implement the framework effectively—essential practices, assessment tools, and planning guidelines. (Find digital versions of assessment, management, and planning tools at scholastic.com/superreaderresources.)

Just as our bones, muscles, and skin give shape and definition to our physical selves, the 7 Strengths shape who we are on the inside. They provide a framework of well-being that enables us to empathize and connect with one another, to face challenges and accept setbacks as we work to overcome them, and to deeply value our cultures, our languages, our lives, our stories and those of others. Reading is a way in, and reading is a way out. Super readers chart their own course, building independence, purpose, and joy every single day. Let's build the super reader community together.

PART I

THE PATH TO CREATING SUPER READERS

The 7 Strengths Framework

CHAPTER 1

WHY SUPER READING MATTERS MORE NOW THAN EVER

"For these are all our children."

—JAMES BALDWIN

Reading is humankind's greatest innovation, touching all corners of independence, purpose, and joy in young people's lives. No matter what tool we use, whether it be a device or a print book or a text message, reading connects us to others and to ourselves. When lonely, we can find someone who speaks to our essential human longings. When in need of a laugh, we can tap into a world of hilarious people. When we want to learn something new or find a way to solve a problem on our own, we can tap into experts from every part of life to guide our way. As much as life has changed since the first edition of this book, and will again in the years to come, reading itself is a constant. The real innovation is not the ways in which advancing technology provides new ways for us to read; it is the reading itself.

We have shared reading experiences with children and teens here in the United States and around the world. We have seen how a child with very few material resources, and who is even hungry for food, will care for and cherish a book in her hand. We have seen how a teen who's struggled with reading her whole life listens to a read-aloud and for the first time feels the sensation of joy in a shared reading experience. We have seen how reading reconnects a child to a parent, helps a solitary child become part of a community, brings courage and strength to a middle schooler facing great challenges. We have seen how a child will read and reread the same book over and over, for "comfort," she says to us. Reading is powerful, precious, and profound.

Still, across the United States there are too many children and young adults who do not see themselves as super readers. Today, this is such an unnecessary tragedy, as we know so much about the joy and power of reading and how to make that joy and power possible for all students, regardless of their life circumstances, their zip code, their socioeconomic status. This innovation can be shared with every child and it must be. Reading opens every child's world. In this book, we use the expression "super reading" to define a very particular kind of reading that is going to give your students a powerful way to read across genres, on all types of platforms, and with the strength to get through the hard parts.

Super reading impacts every aspect of a child's life: the personal, social, academic, and civic, all of them. The child who reads gains comfort, community, and connection to the wider world.

Super reading impacts every aspect of a child's life: the personal, social, academic, and civic, all of them. The child who reads gains comfort, community, and connection to the wider world.

What Is a "Super Reader"?

The super reader is powerful. Regardless of platform (print or digital) or genre (fiction, informational, or poetry), she reads that text with deep comprehension, decoding, and fluency, receiving from it something that informs and possibly inspires. What's more, the super reader can respond to and engage with the text in conversation and writing and use what she learns from the text to make points and answer questions.

The super reader is confident— so confident, in fact, that she is willing to tackle texts that are sometimes difficult for her to comprehend. Like a rock climber on a particularly challenging part of a climbing wall, she savors developing strategies and skills and overcoming obstacles.

The super reader understands the demands of the text—how, for example, its diagrams, charts, graphs, tables, captions, and other features influence the reading process, as do structural elements such as a table of contents, chapters, headings and subheadings, a glossary, and an index. She recognizes literary techniques such as flashbacks, foreshadowing, and stories within stories, as well as literary elements such as metaphors, similes, and idioms, and uses them to engage more actively with the text.

The super reader reads voluminously. She connects with an author, embracing, questioning, and challenging his or her ideas. The super reader notices and admires the author's craft, such as the tone of the piece, the choices of words and phrases, and fluid interplay of dialogue and description, and the way punctuation and white space add meaning.

The super reader is reflective. She questions herself and the text: "How can I become an even better reader?"

The super reader may read in more than one language. She recognizes her home language as an asset and is willing to share her unique perspective with others with confidence and pride.

The super reader is reflective. She questions herself and the text: "How can I become an even better reader?" She is aware of her growth as a reader, setting small and large goals for herself. She understands that becoming a super reader is a continuous process and not an end in itself.

The super reader is a flashlight-in-bed kind of reader, a back-of-the-cereal-box kind of reader, a text-messaging kind of reader, and a comic-book-to-classic-novel kind of reader. The super reader finds solace and comfort in reading. On the loneliest days, reading brings a sense of hope and peace to her life. And, indeed, the super reader loves to read.

The Benefits of Super Reading

Try to imagine a world without reading. Words—reading them, writing them, speaking them—are so central to how most of the world functions that it is nearly impossible for many of us to comprehend what it would mean to live without them. Now, try to imagine what your life would be like if *you* couldn't read. It would be frightening, isolating, disheartening, frustrating, even paralyzing. You might feel like there is no place for you in the world, as if, in the words of Walt Whitman, "the powerful play goes on, and you may contribute a verse," yet you have no verse to contribute.

As teachers, administrators, parents, and community service providers who care about children and their futures, we know much is at stake. Communication is central to how we function in our society. Our innovations in technology, transportation, education, and business stem from the desire to connect individuals to one another with more efficiency and effectiveness. At the heart of communication lies literacy, the skill that makes it all possible.

And so, too, there are the breathtaking learning benefits of voluminous reading:

- developing extensive vocabularies
- having the skills to navigate different kinds of text
- acquiring analytical problem-solving skills
- understanding how reading works—how to orchestrate innumerable skills and strategies in the drive to make meaning
- understanding how writing works—how to spell, punctuate, and create a logically organized sentence, paragraph, and complete, cohesive piece

There are many benefits to super reading, far beyond a test score but, of course, inclusive of all the ways we measure success, including scores. For us to build our Super Reader Classrooms, we need to make a case for them, explain the urgency of this work, why it is so powerful, and why by giving our students this opportunity we are making true freedom and opportunity possible for them. Here are some ways:

Super Reading Translates Into High Achievement

Today, a high school dropout is ineligible for 90 percent of jobs in the United States. According to U.S. Bureau of Labor Statistics (2021), students who drop out of high school are two to three times more likely to be unemployed than those with degrees. We cannot afford to continue to let children grow up without discovering the life-changing effects of joyful learning and a deep engagement with transformative literature.

Reading is a great equalizer that has the power to break down the typical barriers to education.

Reading is a great equalizer that has the power to break down the typical barriers to education. In a study of 6,000 16-year-olds, Sullivan and Brown (2013) found that reading independently was a greater influence on a child's vocabulary, math, and spelling scores than whether their parents held degrees. Eric Litwin (2020) writes "Research by the AAP shows that both poverty and low income result in real hardships… [c]hildren are more likely to have deficits in vocabulary print awareness, language usage, letter-sound relationships, expressive speech, and other essential basic reading skills and knowledge, which make up their reading foundation."

The research is clear: engaged reading translates into high achievement.

Engagement is also essential for meeting the standards. Voluminous independent reading is the best way to meet the goals the standards establish. Though the standards vary from state to state, reading is at the core of each and every one of them (Allington, Billen, & McCuiston, 2015). Literacy is also a key predictor of students' high school graduation rates and college success.

Super Reading Builds Empathy and Understanding

Reading fiction develops empathy—and there's research to prove it. Djikic, Oatley, and Moldoveanu (2013) found that their research participants who were frequent fiction readers scored higher than non-readers on a measure of empathy. Fiction teaches us that it's okay to be different; it can even move us to make societal changes. Annie Murphy Paul articulates the power of cognitive scientist Keith Oatley's research in her *New York Times* op-ed, "Your Brain on Fiction":

> *Brain scans are revealing what happens in our heads when we read a detailed description, an evocative metaphor, or an emotional exchange between characters. Stories…stimulate the brain and even change how we act in life.* (2012)

That's because our brains are, in a sense, fooled—they aren't able to differentiate between the fictional experience and the real-life event. In their research, Kidd and Castano (2013) found that while reading literary fiction, we are forced to use the same mental faculties that help us navigate successful social relationships. When compared with reading nonfiction or no reading at all, groups that read literary fiction were consistently rated as having greater empathy. When we read a narrative through multiple perspectives or infer the thoughts of characters, we are exercising the exact cognitive functions that help us become empathetic beings. These complex relationships and narrative structures are often missing from some types of nonfiction and informational texts.

We have seen through our work at LitWorld that children who read widely are more able to connect with one another. They learn the universality of human emotions through the characters they meet in the pages of books. They learn that people may make mistakes but that mostly, people are trying hard to live well in the world. They learn that most heroes—people who step outside themselves to help others, who are truly kind— are generally ordinary people like all of us and that we are quite capable of being heroes ourselves: heroes of kindness.

Reading keeps us company. Great literature accompanies us through our lifetime. A good book can serve as guide, mentor, friend, and companion through our most exhilarating times and through our loneliest of times.

Super Reading Builds Children's Sense of Self and Emotional Resilience

A kinship with books and stories gives children and adults the skills and emotional strength to believe a dream and make it real. Martin Luther King, Jr. was powerfully influenced by the stories in the Bible when writing his speeches and crafting a life of social change. Whenever Joan Didion is ready to begin writing a new book, she first rereads Joseph Conrad's *Victory* because "it makes it seem worth doing."

Abraham Lincoln did not receive formal schooling. Yet he became a voracious reader, losing himself in a book whenever and wherever he could. It was often said that he could be seen with a book in one hand and an axe in another. Lincoln's love for reading gave him access to worlds that would not have been otherwise possible for him. He credited his love for reading with helping him to become the 16th president of the United States, and he became one of the greatest leaders our nation has ever known. Supreme Court Justice Sonia Sotomayor read Nancy Drew books over and over as a child. She is a Type 1 diabetic, and as a child she was often quite sick. She said that reading Nancy Drew helped her to be strong and brave.

We read "the world," as noted Brazilian educator Paulo Freire (1970) has argued, and we "read the word." We read tablets, sticky notes, text messages, the backs of napkins. We voraciously read street signs and Google searches. We read notes from a friend that make our hearts leap and memos from a colleague that make us stay up late to finish a project. Reading inspires, provokes, motivates, and frustrates. It accompanies us in our every waking moment if we are lucky, and profoundly marginalizes those who are not able to access it.

Reading the world helps us to understand ourselves and find that what makes us special is the essence of who we are and that "the courage in trying" is what makes us truly great."

Super Reading Prepares Children for the Future... Whatever That Might Be!

As we move at light speed through the information age, reading is increasingly important to our personal, social, academic, and civic lives. The first public schools were formed in the United States at the end of the 19th century because government leaders and educators understood that the world was changing and that literacy skills would be important to our future. As we race toward the middle of the 21st century, this has never been more true. As teachers, family members, caregivers, librarians, and out-of-school providers, it has never been more important for us to work together to cultivate strong and confident readers. Reading is humankind's greatest innovation because it is so adaptable to new worlds. Whether we're using tablets, smartphones, or printed books, reading paves the way to new discoveries, new opportunities, and new dimensions in learning. Skills in the new world will be across many devices, and will reflect new technologies that artificial intelligence will bring to us. But the amazing thing is that even in a virtual world collaboration matters. Reading together matters. Communicating and having clarity of thought and mind matters. Being an empathetic colleague matters. Both of us have seen our students grow up and have been fortunate enough to see that the work of literacy lasts them through the years that came after they were in our classrooms. We can see that literacy is the one constant that travels along with them across time, space, and technology advances.

Reading inspires, provokes, motivates, and frustrates. It accompanies us in our every waking moment if we are lucky, and profoundly marginalizes those who are not able to access it.

Raising Super Readers: 10 Fundamental Principles

Ten principles undergird the development of super readers. These are principles we can use to guide our work in building the Super Reader Classroom. And we can share them with our students, and have them engage in building this world together with us.

1 Super readers learn to read by practicing.

Reading is a complex activity involving, among other things, decoding of symbols, phonemic awareness and phonics skills, understanding how stories and information are presented through text, familiarity with vocabulary, and an ability to make literal and metaphoric connections. Effective reading brings all these skills and abilities together to enable us to make meaning from the text.

Not unlike learning to ride a bike, the only way to learn how to draw all these components together in the pursuit of meaning is to dig into text and read—a lot— in school and out.

Each part builds upon another. The adult reading to the child reiterates the flow and power of stories and makes the emotional connection between reading and comfort and happiness. Work with phonics and phonemic awareness enables effective encoding and decoding work, and symbolic recognition and accomplishment. School instruction helps focus on the strategies and techniques to make readers stronger and faster. Conversations at home reinforce curiosity and get to the core of why we read. Reading requires daily practice, which is wonderful because it means that we can help kids become super readers every moment of every day. Interactive reading is also about the reading our students do if they are translanguaging. They may be reading in two languages, or more. They may be reading across multiple texts in different languages. Let us celebrate this and understand that it is what a super reader is so good at: seeing language as having so many cross currents and seeing the home language as an asset!

2 Super readers have a strong foundation in oral language.

Students enter reading with a rich base of linguistic know-how; they understand what language is and how it works. At the same time they are acquiring the technical skills that enable successful reading—with expert teacher guidance—they also need lots and lots of time inside real books, familiarizing themselves with the basics of book handling. All students, especially those who initially find reading challenging, need time to explore real texts and practice reading on their own and with others.

The read-aloud plays a powerful role in the 7 Strengths Framework. It immerses students in literary and informational language, introducing them to rich, wide-ranging vocabulary they aren't likely to encounter anywhere but through books. The child growing up in a biliterate or multiliterate home or school absorbs the rich linguistic input from the read-aloud and transfers it to the work of decoding and meaning-making that reading requires.

Talking about texts is essential, too, because it provides additional meaning-making scaffolds. It deepens, extends, and refines the meaning that students absorb through each read-aloud—and this is especially key for emerging bilinguals and multilinguals. When students talk about texts or collaborate on ideas about texts, it's a pivotal part of the reading experience. Discourse deepens text understanding. It is a vital part of the super reader's learning process. Finally, storytelling itself, a powerful oral skill, is a pivotal foundation for super reading. The writer Eudora Welty said, "Long before I wrote stories, I was listening for them." She remembered sitting under her dining room table while her elders told stories. The input of oral language into the mind and heart of a young person from all those around her is instrumental in strengthening the brain to be ready for reading and to center narrative as a powerful learning source.

3 Super readers understand that reading and writing are mutually beneficial language processes.

Reading is like breathing in, and writing is like breathing out. Reading and writing are complex developmental language processes involving the orchestration and integration of a range of understandings, strategies, skills, and attitudes. Both processes develop as natural extensions of students' need to communicate and make sense of their experiences. Every time we enter a text as a reader, we receive a writing lesson: how to spell, punctuate, use grammar, structure a sentence or paragraph, and organize a text. We also learn the many purposes writing serves and the genres and formats it assumes to serve those purposes (Duke, 2014; Culham, 2010).

What seems to distinguish students who succeed from those who don't is the ability to engage independently in a close analysis of demanding text—and there may be no better way to accomplish that goal than through writing. Writing has a strong and consistently positive impact on reading comprehension. In our Super Reader Classrooms, let us create a synergy between reading and writing: We read to drink in language, and we write to put it into the world. We can do this by writing about reading, by writing our own genres just like those we read; we can do this by savoring the language we find in books and by modeling our writing after our favorite authors. The benefits of writing about text are both abundant and profound—and mirror the kind of thinking we want our students to do when they are reading (Graham & Perin, 2007; Graham & Hebert, 2010):

- Engage in deep thinking about ideas.
- Draw on their own knowledge and experience.
- Consolidate and review information.
- Organize and integrate ideas.
- Be explicit about text evidence.
- Be reflective and reformulate thinking.
- Note personal involvement.
- Capture the reading experience in their own words.

4 Super readers read broadly and deeply for authentic purposes.

Super readers are voracious. They are hungry to read and can read easily across many genres. They are absorbing great amounts of words, images, and text of all kinds. They are not daunted by the complexities of genre, the bold headline of an informational text, the white space of a poem, or the dense volume of a novel. All these things delight and intrigue them. They are not afraid, because they see the purposes for reading in the world and understand the challenges of reading. They have favorites they devour and books they want to reread. They read a magazine while going to their out-of-school activity, social media to find out what their friends are doing, and a long biography of someone they want to know more about in their free time.

They can navigate the unique complexities of each genre. They have questions they want to answer, puzzles they want to solve, and places they want to get to, and they are certain that reading will get them there. They see social media and other online reading experiences also as genres, and they read for the authentic purpose of communication.

5 Super readers have access to many kinds of texts.

All children deserve abundant access to multiple genres and types of text. A child's tastes and interests are changing constantly. Do regular surveys to check in on what students love to read and why. Update the classroom library for your students at least three times a year, introducing new texts, removing texts that are no longer useful, and rearranging how texts are organized. Classroom libraries can be a combination of digital and print in hand. Never underestimate the power of a book—an actual print book—to capture the interest and captivate our young super readers. Browsing and rereading and notating favorite parts are still all easier with print books. But digital libraries can be flagged and tagged, and shared. The ways students access text should be varied and dynamic. Set up systems for students to safely and efficiently access digital material.

In addition to fiction and informational books, include access to comic books, cookbooks, how-to books, celebrity magazines, books on favorite hobbies, graphic novels, and more. Opportunities to examine photographs, diagrams, infographics, and other visual texts bring deeper, richer meaning to what it means to be a reader in the world. The number of books and texts the child is exposed to matters a lot. An essential aspect of becoming a super reader is knowing yourself as a reader—made possible through wide reading driven by access to abundant texts and personal choice.

6 Super readers make choices about what they read.

The research on the impact of student self-selected reading materials is robust and conclusive. Students read more, understand more, and are more likely to continue reading when they have the opportunity to choose what they read (Allington & Gabriel, 2012). Choice is inherently connected to engagement. This engagement with the text is a critical component of a child's education. In a 2014 study of family attitudes and behaviors around reading, 91 percent of children ages 6–17 agreed, "My favorite books are the ones that I have picked out myself" (Scholastic, 2015). A study detailed in *Becoming a Nation of Readers: The Report of the Commission on Reading* (Anderson, Hiebert, Scott, & Wilkinson, 1985) found that: "the 'interestingness' of a text is thirty times more powerful than the readability of text when it comes to comprehension and recall." Nancie Atwell's powerful writing on creating a "literate environment" within her own classrooms shows this in action. By establishing back-and-forth letter writing with her students, Atwell was able to engage in meaningful discussions with each student while also keeping track of their personal thoughts and reading development. Students wrote to Atwell about their frustrations and triumphs, which Atwell would then use to guide them toward texts that might be of use and interest. Even the most reticent of students were finding their own reading material, with confidence and enthusiasm, by the end of the school year (Atwell, 2014).

Each student has unique interests and ideas that will spark his learning journey. As teachers and family members, we must give students the strategies to find texts that will challenge them and the space to grow in the direction they choose. Research shows that when students have more control in choosing their own reading materials, they will select texts that develop their literacy skills—and they will be engaged in the process. This may mean rereading an old favorite one day and trying something new the next. If a student is taught selection strategies and allowed to explore a diverse library, then whatever he chooses will help him along his learning journey.

Super readers need "reading role models."

In addition to helping our students learn to control the specific skills that are necessary for effective reading, we can also help them acquire a deep understanding of what all capable readers do as they work their way through a text. They can see us doing the work of reading with them, from reading aloud to them, to demonstrating struggle with reading to make reading itself visible, to coaching them in their independent reading. We can be more open with students about our own work as readers: building vocabulary and fluency, working on our stamina, and becoming braver and bolder in our growth as readers in what we read throughout the day and in why we make the choices we make. We can share:

- when we are learning vocabulary
- when we are phonemically breaking down sounds in a word
- when reading has felt hard for us
- when reading has felt powerful
- our inner thinking about texts
- what we do when we get to hard parts
- what kinds of choices we make as readers and when
- how we fall in love with authors, genres, and types of text

In general, making visible the strategic actions we employ to guide our own reading is one of the most effective ways to help young readers in our care.

8 Super readers thrive in a collaborative community of readers.

Super readers love to share. And they love to get recommendations and hear what someone else is thinking about a text. Collaboration is about constructing new ideas together about what we read. It is about trusting that the environment is safe for ideas that may not be fully formed but will grow by reading more and more and speaking and listening, too. Speaking and listening are part of the literacy experience, and they are part of how super readers grow.

There are so many ways to set up collaborative environments in the Super Reader Classroom. The collaboration can be through technology, connecting as reading pals, or through a face-to-face club. However we set this up, we have to acknowledge that reading alone can still be in community with others. So even if we are sitting alone to do our reading, we can hear the voices and support of others in our minds.

9 Super readers develop the strengths and skills to read by spending time reading independently.

Students who read independently perform better in school. According to Beers and Probst, "Independent reading is not simply reading independently, free from the teacher's control and direction—it is reading that leads to independence, reading that may generate new and previously unimagined ideas about who we are, who we might become, how we might function in the world. It is that sort of reading that might solve the problems our students, as they have poignantly told us, want to address. It is that sort of reading that might answer the questions that matter to them" (Beers & Probst, 2020).

The amount of free reading done outside of school has consistently been found to relate to growth in vocabulary, reading comprehension, verbal fluency, and general information (Anderson, Wilson, & Fielding, 1988; Guthrie & Greaney, 1991; Taylor, Frye, & Maruyama, 1990). Students who read independently become better readers, score higher on achievement tests in all subject areas, and have greater content knowledge than those who do not (Cunningham & Zibulsky, 2014; Krashen, 2004).

10 Super readers are joyful readers.

Pleasure is always at the heart of engaged super reading. Children who read avidly with delight and joy understand themselves as readers, know their own reading interests and passions, and, as a result, are adept at finding the texts that maximize reading delight. Super reading programs that invite reading choice and promote reading pleasure give rise to super readers who not only read but also, more importantly, want to read. Reading isn't always easy. Engaging with difficulty can also feel joyful. A super reader is not afraid of difficult text and does not blame herself when the reading gets hard. The super reader finds joy in the struggle and understands it is part of the journey.

Next Steps to Building a Super Reader Classroom

We hope that by now you are convinced of the need to develop the super reader in every child. But you may be asking yourself, "How do we do this? How can I contribute to this worthy endeavor?" Chapter 2 explains the 7 Strengths Framework, the thinking behind it, and the power it holds to create super readers.

THE 7 STRENGTHS FRAMEWORK: INDEPENDENCE, PURPOSE, AND JOY

"We can read ourselves into a better future."

—MALCOLM MITCHELL

In the first edition of *Every Child A Super Reader*, our mission was to convince the reader of the power in a new idea. We believed in the 7 Strengths wholeheartedly, knowing it was transformational for our students. We asked: "How do we help all students, regardless of personal circumstance or zip code, achieve in the classroom and beyond?" Now, after five years of using the 7 Strengths in practice, and seeing its profound impact on students around the world, our mission shifts. Now we ask: "How can we best help all children become world changers in their schools, homes, and communities?" In practice, we have learned that the 7 Strengths is not a strategy for some students, but something every child and adult can use not only to grow as learners, but to love the person they see in the mirror, and to be in the world with empathy and care for others.

The research-based 7 Strengths Framework has proven itself effective in practice: We know what it looks like. As it's come alive, the framework has demonstrated not only its success, but its flexibility. When LitCamp was reinvented for online contexts during the pandemic, it was able to pivot seamlessly because of the strengths and the way children use them for support and grounding in a complex world. The 7 Strengths

Framework has become a movement, propelled by millions of kids around the country who have academic breakthroughs using this model, and who hold fast to the strengths as a North Star in unprecedented times. We have seen the 7 Strengths help teachers feel hopeful about influencing their students' lives and talk about and teach reading as an empathy tool for creating consideration for others. We have seen the 7 Strengths give students a voice, assure their sense of self, and strengthen their drive to change the world.

The framework inspires a sense of safety and well-being as readers build lifelong connections to textual experiences and higher-level thinking skills. The 7 Strengths connects reading to the inner life of the student. The student learns how reading can connect to his deepest experience as a human being.

The first three strengths—Belonging, Friendship, and Kindness—are about honing the self, exploring the internal qualities and capacities that bring us to community. We have to work on these strengths; they are not a given. Reading helps us to learn about belonging, friendship, and kindness in the pages of stories. We also learn more about these strengths by being part of a community of super readers. The fourth strength, Curiosity, delves into how each student takes on a stance of wonder and inquiry, and how our classrooms can reflect that, too.

With the last three strengths—Confidence, Courage, and Hope—we reach outward. The strengths are exhilarating. They are building within us the capacity to be community members, and even more, to be leaders. Many of the LitWorld and LitClub members who

were the creators of the 7 Strengths are now leaders in their own home communities. They practiced leadership through the strengths. Let's take this framework and build a world of community together, for every reader, for every student. We can do it!

That being said, except for the first strength, Belonging, and the last, Hope, you can feel free to move the strengths around as needed or, if desired, to create the kind of environment you want and need. The 7 Strengths are meant to be flexible and meet the needs of your students. And sometimes that flexibility is in response to an urgent need your students have to bond and connect, and other times, we might want to connect the strengths to a unit we are doing (let's say a science unit or an inquiry unit we want to connect with one of the outward-facing strengths). The only two we want to always see as bookends are Belonging and Hope because they anchor us, and help us fly.

In 2007, we founded LitWorld, an organization that provides transformational literacy experiences for children across the United States and in more than 60 countries. Some of our first LitClub and LitCamp graduates who pioneered the 7 Strengths are the first members of their families to attend college; others are taking on local civic leadership roles. The 7 Strengths were built in collaboration with the young people in our LitWorld communities. We saw that young people across the world were full of the strengths that defined them—their family stories, their home languages, their cultures, their ancestors and elders. All of this was what made them powerful, and yet there was no language to describe this. We asked them, with us, to rethink the way we read the world. We asked them to begin with what made them strong. And country to country, language to language, the 7 Strengths began to emerge. In every language, in every community, children and teens started to bloom when talking about reading, writing, and storytelling through the lens of this framework.

The 7 Strengths Create a Culturally Responsive Reading World

Rudine Sims Bishop (1990) described the ways in which literature can serve as windows, sliding glass doors, and mirrors. Books can become windows, offering "views of worlds that may be real or imagined, familiar or strange." Readers can then treat these windows as sliding glass doors by walking through them and into the world created by the author. These same windows can also serve as mirrors, reflecting the readers' lives and experiences back to them "as part of the larger human experience." In the Super Reader Classroom, we must provide reading experiences and texts that reflect the lived experiences of all our children. Walter Dean Myers often spoke of how he had never seen himself as he was in the pages of a book, and that this is why he began writing his own books for children and young adults. We don't want our students to have to write their way into a world in which there is no one who feels or looks or sounds like them. Let's bring all the voices into our rooms; let's make those voices central to our teaching and our work.

Whether at home with children or in the classroom, let us prioritize the mirrors and windows library, the mirrors and windows world, the mirrors and windows conversations in which every child can find herself and also see out to the larger world.

Christopher Myers, in a *New York Times* op-ed, describes how not having abundant access to diverse texts results in children of color who "recognize the boundaries being imposed upon their imaginations, and are certain to imagine themselves well within the borders they are offered, to color themselves inside the lines."

Every child deserves to know she belongs to the world of reading and the world of writing. Whether White or Black, Latino or Asian, boy or girl or nonbinary—everyone and anyone can, will, and should benefit from a library as diverse as the world we live in. The world is stretching its wings and at long last recognizing that the power of story is central to our human experience. Certainly all children can relate to a good story whether or not the character looks like them. But there is no question that we hunger to see ourselves, to have reflections that we can call our own. The Super Reader Classroom can and must reflect the multiplicity of languages in the texts we read, the books we browse, the ways we invite our students to give book talks and presentations. Home languages must be centered, beloved, and celebrated, in how we promote translanguaging and how we feature multilingual texts across all genres. This is advocacy work we must do and continue to do so every child can see themselves here, and in the future, as leaders and creators.

The 7 Strengths are about building self, community, and world connecting toward a sense of well-being and centeredness in life and learning. They are about a positive, asset-based approach to how students learn, framing each individual as someone who is bringing a huge wealth of possibility with them to their learning. And finally, the strengths are about how students both see and approach text itself when learning to read and reading to learn, with each of the strengths as guideposts for how they can tackle texts and become lifelong readers.

Let's take a deep dive into the 7 Strengths.

 ## BELONGING: Being a valued, cherished member

For a child to flourish, she must know that she is a valued member of a community and that her unique voice is respected. When a child feels as though she doesn't belong; she becomes removed; she disappears from group conversations; she may appear resistant. Our core sense of belief in ourselves stems from the knowledge that others believe in us, too. Both the classroom and the home can be places for comfort and growth, assuring the child of her value as an individual so that she can go out and affect change in the world.

A child who belongs is known by others. Her reading preferences are known. She knows the reading preferences of others. She is celebrated when she takes a step forward. She celebrates others. Children hunger to belong, to clubs, to groups. Reading is designed to build a social community and super readers are made by building a social community around them. The child is also someone who can change and will be supported in that change and growth.

What you choose to read to students is critical. If a young girl never reads a book with a female main character, how can she take a leading role in her own life? If bilingual students only read books in English, how will they learn that their culture and language are valued? Activities and discussions involving students must reflect their own agency as community members. Our language as teachers must firmly plant students in their growth as powerful readers and writers.

Students thrive as readers when surrounded by reading material and the language of literacy. Books and talk about books help establish a reading or "scholarly" culture in the home, one that persists from generation to generation, largely independent of education and class. This promotes the skills and knowledge that foster literacy and numeracy and, thus, lead to lifelong academic advantages (Evans et al., 2010). When we create a sense of independence, purpose, and joy in our classrooms, and we welcome our students to it, there is already an atmosphere of belonging. But best of all is when we say: "I see you, I hear you, and I honor you." That's the best way to create a place of belonging for every student entering the classroom.

Students self-identify as readers who belong to a larger reading community whose members know books, talk about books, share books, and love books.

FRIENDSHIP: Having close, trusting relationships and personal connections to others—learning to interact in positive, productive ways

Whether in the home, classroom, or workplace, being able to listen, speak, and connect with others is extremely important. Friendship is a strength that fosters within students a deeper understanding of themselves. Navigating friendships can be difficult, yet it is a powerful and necessary tool that must be cultivated. "Friendship is a highly complex and emotionally demanding transaction and meeting the challenges of friendship requires emotional awareness and applied strengths" (O'Grady, 2012). Psychologists from the University of Illinois and the University of Pennsylvania found that there is a strong correlation between health, happiness, and friendship (Diener & Seligman, 2002).

Being a super reader should not be lonely. We learn better together than by ourselves (Schaps, 2009). Reading is enhanced when we recommend books to one another, when we trust one another, and when we support one another through the hard parts of reading. A super reader mindset is protective not only for academic progress but for mental health as well, which is increasingly a problem.

Yet, in a classroom that focuses on individual learning, friendship can too often be seen as a distraction, something that can get you into trouble. Because of this, students have not always been explicitly taught how to engage in friendships. Super readers cultivate relationships around the telling and receiving of stories and by sharing them. From great literature, they learn about the imperfections of relationships. They empathize with characters and reflect on their own relationships in light of what they have read.

KINDNESS: Being compassionate toward others, expressing tenderness that has an impact, near and far

Kindness is the heartbeat of our civil society, and it is what we remember most in both the challenging and joyous times of our lives. In fact, "…scientific studies prove there are many physical, emotional, and mental health benefits associated with kindness" (Currie, 2014). Kindness prevents bullying, fortifies every single human being, and powers us forward when we are faced with adversity.

Students can internalize the lessons of kindness from the books they read. They can learn from these stories that being considerate of others goes much further than simply looking out for yourself. Families, librarians, and teachers can make every effort to choose texts that promote active explorations of kindness, whether they be fiction or biographies or examples of kindness in social media posts, and can be used as platforms to hold discussions about humanity. A community *without* kindness will not succeed; it is only by working with one another, instead of against, that we can harness the positive energy of our combined agency.

CURIOSITY: Fostering a willingness to explore new territory and test new theories

Students who ask questions are proactively engaged in their environments and learn to anticipate both problems and solutions. They are hungry for knowledge and for all the ways the world works.

We must create environments that are open and hospitable to the kinds of unique, interesting responses students have to texts and in conversations. Curiosity is a spark that must be fueled by the affirmation of wonderings.

Reading creates curiosity, and books should be seen as a launching pad for further inquiry. Our conversations around texts must expand beyond character analysis to encourage students to look out into the world and to be more and more curious about human nature and about themselves navigating the world around them. Project-based learning allows students to follow lines of inquiry of their own choosing, resulting in higher engagement and stronger results. A focus on asking open-ended questions cultivates students' curiosity and fosters an attitude of being "forever learners."

CONFIDENCE: Thinking independently, expressing ideas, and pushing through the hard parts with resilience

Confidence is a garden that must be cultivated consistently through the small challenges and triumphs of each day. The student arrives with many preconceived ideas of what she can't do. Perhaps reading has felt like an insurmountable challenge. But there is something she feels confident about. The Super Reader Classroom will bring that out. And we can use that feeling to amplify her sense of confidence as a learner.

In our classrooms, let's be on the lookout for moments of confidence and call those out. If a student is encoding or decoding text, tackling a challenging vocabulary word, getting to a deeper understanding of a complex text, writing about reading in a way that seizes the imagination of others—all of this is worthy of a moment to stop and say, "I am so proud to see you doing this work. This is confidence work!"

A super reader is able to approach any situation knowing that she has the tools for success within herself. Let us create a genuinely affirmational and inclusive environment that allows students to feel confident as readers, thinkers, and learners.

COURAGE: Having the strength to stand up for yourself, for others, and to take action when it is needed

Super reading helps our students find ways to navigate a world that can seem confusing and not always at all hospitable to young people. In the pages of books and magazines our students can watch characters, both real and imagined, navigate hard worlds and triumph. They can also see how courage can be practiced, and learned. Courage also is seen in literature as not only the kind that requires a cape and superpowers but as a tender form of grace and empathy. Characters such as Juice in *Just Juice* by Karen Hesse or Mia in *Front Desk* by Kelly Yang reveal small steps of courage that benefit those around them. We can also see courage as what it takes to become a super reader. Encoding and decoding hard words are one thing that sometimes require a form of learning courage, as is breaking down meaning in text and comprehending, sharing, and raising your voice with an idea, even if it's not what everyone else seems to be thinking.

In our classrooms, with this strength front forward, we can talk about what it takes to feel like you can share in your own true voice, you can agree or disagree with a friend about a book or something you are learning about, and more. We can use the strength of courage as a lens by which we can think about writing in response to reading: becoming fearless in how we react to books we read and news, articles, and blogs. Speaking and listening are all part of the super reader experience, so there is courage in this too: courageous listening and courageous speaking. Listening with an open heart and mind and not self-judging when someone's ideas are different but using your courage strength to open up to other people's mindsets. And similarly, to speak with an open mind and heart, with courage to share one's ideas while not needing or wanting others to have to agree or approve, but to have the fearlessness of having a voice. All of these ways of experiencing courage lead to the world-changing element of the strengths. By visiting with characters in fiction and nonfiction, our students are building examples of lives that are led with dignity and where people are taking a risk for the benefit of others. That is a really big idea that literature helps us to absorb and make personal. If we just watch the news or see things from afar, we think we are not capable of being those people who stand up for others, who take care of each other, who speak up when there is injustice. But super reading helps our young people enter a world where they can take action, too— where their courage can change the world.

HOPE: Thinking optimistically and believing that today's efforts will produce good things in the future for yourself and the world

In the work we do, we are always inspired and motivated by how our students find hope even in the darkest of times. The seeking of hope is a condition of childhood and young adulthood. We as adults like to call it "resilience" or "grit," but here in the super reader world we call it what it most simply reveals itself to be: hope. Literature has a remarkable capacity to help us give children the idea that they can turn their dreams into reality. The child who is reading Peter. Reynolds' book *Say Something* sees herself as having agency and power to have a voice and make a small change that makes a big difference. Reading *Layla and the Bots* by Vicky Fang gives the child the idea that she can really impact the outcomes of people's lives with design thinking. Reading *The Hunger Games* by Suzanne Collins gives the young person the idea that being strong and visionary as a young person can remake a world entirely. By reading narrative nonfiction our students can learn and grow, becoming knowledgeable about science and history and other areas of study that make hope lively and real. From the earliest ages, students can explore their wonderings and ideas by becoming armed with the facts and resources they need to build a life of consequence. Finally, super reading makes it possible for our students to see the world beyond their own communities and homes. Nothing is impossible. Super readers are eager to play their role in making the impossible possible.

The 7 Strengths

BELONGING: Being a valued, cherished member of a larger community

FRIENDSHIP: Having close, trusting relationships and personal connections to others—learning to interact in positive, productive ways

KINDNESS: Being compassionate toward others; expressing tenderness that has an impact, near and far

CURIOSITY: Fostering a willingness to explore new territory and test new theories

CONFIDENCE: Thinking independently, expressing ideas, and pushing through the hard parts with resilience

COURAGE: Having the strength to stand up for yourself, for others, and to take action when it is needed

HOPE: Thinking optimistically and believing that today's efforts will produce good things in the future for yourself and the world

Top 10 Ways to Nurture a Super Reader

Here are some tips for developing super readers in school and at home. Feel free to share some of these with students' family members as you see fit.

1 Value students and their stories.

You can make students' reading futures brighter by making it clear that their stories matter to the life of the classroom, home, and community.

The 7 Strengths help students access their stories through connections to texts they read or that are read aloud to them and in conversations with trusted adults in their lives. Use these questions to prompt such conversations:

Strength	Questions to Elicit Stories From Students
Belonging	• When have you felt you were part of a group or community? • What kinds of communities have you read about lately?
Friendship	• When have you felt a connection to another person? • When has a friendship from a book inspired you?
Kindness	• When have you reached out to others? • What books are you reading (or are we reading) that show kindness?
Curiosity	• What questions do you have? • What are you wondering about in something you are reading or have read lately?
Confidence	• When have you felt bold? • Have you ever read something that made you feel more confident?
Courage	• What makes you feel brave? • What stories have you read that inspired you to be courageous?
Hope	• What are your dreams? • What new ideas, hopes, and dreams has your reading inspired?

2 Invite students into a safe and supportive reading environment.

You and your students' families provide the security and support they need to take risks to grow as a readers. Let students know you value their development as readers by creating:

- cozy physical spaces as havens for reading and rereading favorite books
- a quiet corner where they can always find solitude
- baskets where they can keep favorite books

Encourage families to value reading of all kinds—even reading we don't always consider "serious," such as the backs of cereal boxes and comic books. Make sure students know it's okay to read easier books and to reread them, because it's something super readers do all the time, plus it builds stamina and confidence.

The language you and family members use to invite students to join you in a reading environment will make a lifelong impact. Use comments like:

- I value you as a reader.
- Let's read together. I love to read with you!
- I sometimes struggle as a reader, too, and want you to know that it is totally normal.
- I see you rereading favorite books. That is a great thing for a super reader to do!
- Tell me what would make our home more comfortable for you as a reader.

3 Dedicate daily time for students to read for pleasure.

The more students are encouraged to read for pleasure, the more likely they are to become engaged readers (Guthrie, 2004) and develop identities as readers. In *You Gotta BE the Book: Teaching Engaged and Reflective Reading With Adolescents*, Jeffrey Wilhelm (1996) advocates for middle school students to have freedom to read "fun" books in class. When he allowed students to choose books themselves, he found they became more excited about reading and read more. Donalyn Miller (2009) found that when she provided time for her sixth graders to read the books they selected they read 40 to 50 books a year—far more than they had read in previous years. Harvey, et. al (2021) describe the importance of daily reading in sparking students' launch into what they call "the Virtuous Cycle" of progress in which reading volume, success, confidence, and capability grow together in an upward spiral.

Encourage families to create uninterrupted time every day for pleasure reading at home, even if it's only 10 or 15 minutes. If necessary, they can set a timer and say something like, "Let's read together for six minutes tonight!" to show students that they read for pleasure, too. Pass the message along that family members shouldn't limit themselves in terms of what they read—from the sports section to the comics to a recipe, they should read what they like to read. If some family members don't like to read, or struggle with reading, they can talk about that with their child, and say: "Let's work on liking it more together!"

4 Read aloud, read aloud, read aloud.

Reading aloud to children is a research-proven strategy for helping them learn to read, which may seem counterintuitive. After all, if the child is not doing the reading herself, how can she become better at it? Because she is marinating in language. She is swimming in a delightful bath of words. Reading aloud also inspires children to pick up books on their own and exposes them to lots of new vocabulary and a range of texts they may not be able to read on their own. In short, reading aloud inspires them to become super readers.

Encourage family members to make time for reading aloud each day. If they are too tired in the evening, they can read aloud in the morning. Or they can ask their child to read aloud to them while they are preparing dinner. Family members can read aloud during bath time (think waterproof books!) or while waiting on line at the store. Encourage family members to have a book with them to read aloud wherever they go.

5 Honor students' own varied reading choices.

If our goal is to develop lifelong readers, let us not judge their quirky, funny, eccentric choices. Students will learn how powerfully books can speak to them, entertain them, instruct them, and help to build their identities as super readers if they are allowed to make their own choices and are made to feel good about those choices. Make sure families give their children that chance by having great book/home access opportunities, both in print and digitally. Send books between home and school every day and let those options be abundant so that you are fostering a whole family experience with reading.

6 Provide daily access to books and stories in all forms, genres, and platforms.

It has been said of dancers, athletes, musicians, and other experts that just a day away from their practice makes them rusty. The same can be said of readers. In your communications home, make sure your students' family members know that you count reading as everything from the cereal box to a recipe to the text message. It will be fun to have family members count minutes and make sure those countable minutes value all the "ordinary" things readers do in everyday life. All texts are, in so many ways, helping students become super readers.

7 Champion skillful rereading.

Each time a super reader rereads a book, it is a new experience because he is constantly growing and changing as a reader. Although the words on the page do not change, the reader does because his interpretations change each time he revisits a favorite book. Encourage students to reread, letting them know that rereading builds stamina, deepens comprehension, and enhances knowledge. If students are rereading voluntarily, do not assume it is because they want reading to feel "easy." Rereading takes work. Just as we may prepare a favorite dish again and again to become a better cook, so, too, a child may read a favorite book again and again to become a better reader. Also, a student who is rereading may be reading as a writer, as an "encoder" rather than just as a "decoder." Highlight for your students that super writers are always rereading for inspiration and for examples of extraordinary sentence and grammatical structures, and how the writer took them on this awesome journey.

8 Help students see authors as real people making real decisions.

Invite students to look at examples of author's notes, forewords, acknowledgment pages, and endnotes in books, as well as author websites and blogs. By doing that, they will see authors as real people. When reading together, stop and use the author's name to describe a beautiful craft element, or to wonder about how he or she researched that part of the book.

Encourage students to reach out to authors personally. In this era of social media, authors are far more accessible than ever before, and even a brief reply is thrilling—and will fuel their desire to read and write.

9 Value students' talk and exchanges of ideas.

Talking about what we've read is an important part of being in a community of readers. Whether they're at the dinner table or in front of classmates, students need space to share their ideas and hear the ideas of others. Why? First and foremost, it shows students that their words are valuable. It also allows students to process how they are learning. As they share ideas, they develop and refine those ideas. Reading is essential, but reading and talking is where all the magic happens—the greatest learning. Ask open-ended questions such as, "What are you wondering? What are you thinking? What are you imagining?" rather than starting and ending with definitive statements. Encourage students to express opinions of books they are reading (including when they don't like what they are reading) as these opinions are also the sign that you are cultivating super readers who have perspectives on their reading lives and are keen to share them.

10 Be a reading role model.

All of the adults in students' lives have a wonderful opportunity to model super reading for children. Students should see us reading to learn and reading for pleasure. Whether we are reading a book, the morning paper, a recipe, or a website on some topic that interests us, students should see us reading! And it is okay if they see us struggle. We read above our "level," below our "level," and right at our "level." We read "uphill" books and "downhill" books. We read jokes from a friend and subway maps. In fact, "parents and other adult family members—along with teachers and school librarians—are the top people in children's lives who encourage them to read books for fun" (Scholastic Report, 2018). In this age of tablets and smartphones, it is harder to be conspicuous reading role models for students. They often can't detect if we are actually reading or just playing a game. For that reason, encourage family members to share what they're reading with their child. ("I love this funny article I am reading." or "I got this message from my boss that was hard to understand, so I'm rereading it.") The key here for all reading role models: Be yourself. Students will see reading as a part of your life, even when reading feels challenging, and understand that super readers in the world are constantly growing, changing, and improving.

Next Steps in the Journey

Together, the 7 Strengths provide a framework for valuing the child, for welcoming her into a community of readers, and for developing her desire and skill to speak and act in the world. In Chapters 3 through 9, we look at each strength up close. We speak to why each strength matters, what it looks like in practice, and how to use a favorite book to deepen students' understanding of the strength. The strengths can accompany our students for a lifetime of reading. Let's explore them deeply here so we can give them this gift, to be used in all circumstances, everywhere they go.

CHAPTER 3

STRENGTH ONE: BELONGING

"It is really hard to be lonely very long in a world of words. Even if you don't have friends somewhere, you still have language, and it will find you and wrap its little syllables around you, and suddenly there will be a story to live in."

—NAOMI SHIHAB NYE

Jaslyn was facing a new school year. The first day of third grade was coming soon. Her mother helped her pick out her first-day outfit and purchase a new purple lunch box. She was ready. When the day came for the class lists, she bounced eagerly into the car. "Who do you hope you see on that list, Jaslyn?" her mother asked. Jaslyn's response was quick. "Ariana—and Dominic and Ella! I crossed my fingers and toes and wished last night that we are in class together," she said. "Why?" inquired her mom. "It's so much better when you know your friends are going to be with you. It's a safe feeling. Plus, we like to work together. We trade books when we like one and we like to read each other's stories. Being with them makes me feel happy."

When Jorge started his after-school program, he was learning English for the first time. He was eight years old. He was from Guyana, and he was also deaf. His after-school leader invited him to share what he loved to do back at home and he said that he was a good caretaker of animals. She invited him to create a basket of animal books with her and to become the "animal book expert" for his classmates. That helped Jorge feel a sense of belonging with his classmates, who soon crossed all language barriers to find out the latest animal he was reading about.

Belonging to a community is as basic a human need as nourishment and shelter. We are wired to need each other, and it fuels our learning to be in a safe, supportive belonging community. Children thrive when they belong and when they feel safe and surrounded by a community that values their presence. What better opportunity to provide this healthy sense of belonging than in a classroom? When the classroom stakeholders—students, teachers, school staff members, and families—come together, that kind of community is bound to flourish.

What does this have to do with reading? First, belonging to a community and feeling safe, positive, and happy in it helps students become empowered and more connected to the work that is required within the class. They'll be excited to do the reading work because they feel valued and feel seen. Secondly, when the community identifies itself by its very nature as a group of avid readers and hard-working authors, children feel a sense of growing definition of themselves and can say, "I am a member of this mighty group that so values super reading and writing, so therefore, I too am a super reader!"

Why Belonging Matters

There is strong evidence that having human connections and being successful at school are related. We have decades of research that suggests having at least one strong and stable relationship with a supportive adult is a key factor in helping children cope with high-stress situations (Harvard University's Center on the Developing Child, 2015). While that relationship is often found in the home, it can also be found in school. The teacher-student relationship is an ideal support for those students who may lack a sense of belonging in the home, and it can also give children

who do enjoy a rich family life an even stronger sense of belonging, particularly when families and teachers work together. Relationships matter a great deal in the Super Reader Classroom. The teacher serves as coach and guide, nurturing the child's assets.

In Bergin and Bergin's review of attachment research in education (2009), they argue that secure attachments to teachers, administrators, and other students are the foundation of students' social and emotional well-being in school. Students who develop meaningful attachments to teachers and classmates also develop meaningful attachments to the work of the classroom. Those attachments provide the foundation for a student to identify as an engaged and capable reader, which is so crucial to reading success. Super readers need to belong to a community of people who value who they are, their ideas, and their personal journeys as learners.

What You Can Do to Promote Belonging in Your Classroom

♥ Make heart maps.

The great writer, educator, poet, and leader Georgia Heard has shared with us her beautiful heart maps (2016). Heart maps have become a signature way for the teams at LitWorld to build a sense of belonging in students as readers and learners, all across the year. A heart map is a graphic representation of things that students hold dear in their hearts, or things they are wondering about deeply. Make the shape of a heart out of paper (or online in their tablets or phones) large enough for students to fill it up with writing (or online on their tablets or phones). Have students divide their hearts as they wish and write things that are "in their heart"—people, pets, books, and ideas that they cherish—in those sections. They can write about and also look for books about the things they included on their heart maps. You can use heart maps in many ways to get conversations going in the classroom (and at home). For example, you can invite students to create heart maps of:

- people who have inspired them
- places that have touched them or that they wish to return to
- their hopes and dreams
- their wonderings

By sketching heart maps frequently throughout the year, students can use them as conversation starters with others, to find a place of belonging in the classroom, and to center others' ideas.

Create digital spaces for students and families.

Creating digital spaces for students and families promotes collaboration and a sense of belonging. Students can write about reading or respond to longer conversations about a favorite text or group of texts. Creating a sense of belonging through the virtual community helps families join in, too, to see what students are working on and to watch the reading identity grow and blossom in each child. Some possible prompts to encourage the spirit of belonging may include:

- How do you feel you are growing as a reader this week?
- What titles or types of books can you recommend to friends?
- What kinds of affirmations can you share with your reading friends?

Personalize the classroom library.

The crown jewel in a community of super readers is the classroom library, both on- and offline. The collection owned and cared for by the community should reflect the work and preferences of members of that community, which means that your classroom library will change every year and also throughout the year. The classroom library should be referred to as "ours," and the care and curating of it should be the responsibility of everyone who uses it. Make sure all students are familiar with the various sections of their library. Create a sense of ownership by inviting students to add books from home to the collection or request additions or add to the collection themselves with books from home or books they've written. Decide on key points in the year when students can create new baskets or files, and create new categories (for example, stories with courageous characters and Carmen Agra Deedy books). Create a place where students can make recommendations to friends near the bins or online.

Value, promote, and actively advocate for powerful diversity in the classroom library. Every student should be able to see his own self or hear a voice that speaks her language in the pages of books as well as hearing many other voices and perspectives. Cecilia Espinosa and Laura Ascenzi-Moreno (2021) note that "[p]aying attention to the linguistic landscapes of your school is important because it sends a powerful message to students and families that their languages and linguistic repertoires are valued." Display and honor books, stories, and information that reflect the lives of people around the globe, people of all nationalities, cultures, ethnic groups, gender perspectives, and linguistic backgrounds. In a "belonging" library, students can say, "I see myself in this collection" and "I see a world I want to know about."

Design an environment that supports belonging.

Make the wall space come alive with students' work. Create a world of belonging with a bulletin board called "Welcome to My World," where each child gets to imagine/wonder/remember/observe the kind of world she wants us to know is hers. She can bring images, photos, art, and found objects from her life at home and school to post on the board. This can also be done virtually if you have access to Internet tools that other students can visit and browse.

Belonging classrooms encourage and support a lot of talk, and that talk is trusting and safe. Readers can jumpstart and facilitate conversation; they can help other readers go deeper in conversation.

We can also build our belonging communities through the read-aloud. Books such as *The Recess Queen, Wonder, My People, Weslandia, Sitti's Secrets*, and Walt Whitman's *Leaves of Grass* all point out the important theme of belonging. *The Recess Queen* is specifically about the child who recognizes her need to be part of a community of her peers; *My People* speaks eloquently through the poetry of Langston Hughes about what it means to fight a fierce battle for belonging; *Weslandia* is an enchanted look at another universe where one can belong in new ways; *Sitti's Secrets* is about how belonging can reach across oceans; and *Leaves of Grass* points to the radical voice that Whitman shared in the 1800s that spoke to democracy and the ultimate notion that belonging is for everyone. Each of those texts relates directly to the concept of belonging and can help students construct their own ideas about belonging to their family, community, school, and wider world. By affirming the growth of the child every day, week, and month, we are saying: "Yes, you belong here as a reader." Examples of what we mean by that include:

- I admire how you've been spending more time reading these days.
- I notice that you are the kind of reader who likes to read with a partner.
- It was so exciting to see you take a new step as a reader today.
- I observed that you like to reread familiar texts, and that is something great readers do.

To create a sense of belonging for all readers, reading time should include plenty of opportunities for students to talk with one another. Ask the following questions—and pose them for students to ask one another:

- What book did you fall in love with this week?
- What kind of reading most lights your fire?
- Where did reading feel hard, and how can we be of help?

Belonging classrooms encourage and support a lot of talk, and that talk is trusting and safe. Readers can jump-start and facilitate conversation; they can help other readers go deeper in conversation. Peer conversations in partnerships, small groups, and whole-class scenarios support the kind of deeper thinking and analysis needed for super reading. In belonging classrooms, students consult with one another to choose reading materials. They invite each other to work through the hard parts of texts together and sit and do the work of close readers when texts push them beyond their levels of understanding. They use language like the following:

- I am enthusiastic about what you said about...
- I learned _____ from you as a reader today.
- I want to add on to what you said about that passage.
- I hear you, and I have another point of view to contribute.
- I love that book, too!
- I have a different opinion, and I want to deepen our conversation by sharing it.

Community River Maps

By incorporating information about your reading community on a Community River Map, you can foster a sense of belonging and recognize what connects super readers and what makes each one of them unique.

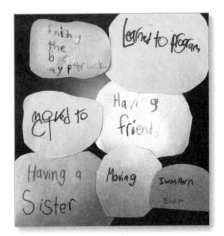

Directions

1. Introduce the lesson by saying:

   Readers become stronger when they belong to a strong reading community. Today's lesson will help us learn more about each other. This will help us grow closer as a group and see ways that we can support each other as readers.

2. Give each student a stack of paper "stones" (paper cut into circles). On each paper stone, ask students to write their name on the back. On the front, they should write one thing that is important to them by completing sentence starters, such as:

   - *I like to learn about…*
   - *My favorite author is…*
   - *My favorite genre (type of book) is…*
   - *Something that makes me happy is…*
   - *When I read, I like to…*
   - *Something I like to do for fun is…*
   - *I can help classmates with…*

3. Create a "river" for students to place their stones. (This can be a long piece of paper taped on the wall.)

4. Once students have incorporated all of their stones, have them peruse the river and look at the contributions of their classmates. Emphasize things that many students share. To spark conversation, you can ask:

- *Looking at our Community River Map, what do you notice that we have in common?*
- *How does discovering things we share in common help us as a reading community?*
- *How does discovering what makes us unique help us as a reading community?*
- *What prompts did some of us choose? Why do you think so?*
- *What prompts were less popular? Why do you think so?*
- *How can all of these discoveries help us grow and strengthen our reading community?*

5. Keep the Community River Map up for a few days. Then take down the stones and distribute them to the owners. On a large piece of paper with their names showing, have students draw a picture of themselves and glue the stones to the poster. Invite them to add more stones if they wish. Hang the poster so students can learn about each other as individuals to support their work together as readers. Encourage students to connect with each other. For example, they might use this information to share books that might interest other group members, work together in interest groups, and go to "experts" in the class on various topics.

Actions for Promoting Belonging in the Super Reader Classroom

Book Baskets	Create personalized book baskets or online folders for each student to curate his or her own reading collection.
Heart Maps	Have each student draw a heart on a sheet of paper, and then fill it with words and images that represent places where and times when he or she has felt a deep sense of belonging.
Belonging Bulletin Board	Create a personalized corner of a bulletin board in the classroom for each student in the class to share about his or her passions.
Welcome to My World	Students can use their imagination or things they've observed to not only think about the world now, but to share positive things they would like to add to or change about the world today. They can then conceptualize this world on a poster board and share as a group.
Hand Circle	Create a circle of hand prints on a large poster board. Have students place their hands on the paper to form a circle and trace the outline of their hands. Within the circle they have created, they can write words that reflect a peaceful, collaborative, affirmational environment.

INTERACTIVE READING LESSON

All Because You Matter

by Tami Charles
illustrated by Bryan Collier

Summary: In *All Because You Matter* by Tami Charles, a young boy begins to understand the innate and eternal value his life holds and why his existence is, and has always been, so important to his family, to his community, and to the world.

Before Reading	**Discuss Belonging:**

Before Reading

Discuss Belonging:
- What people, groups, communities, activities, or places give you a sense of belonging?
- How might a sense of belonging help you? What kinds of actions do others take that make you feel you belong?
- How would you show a new friend or family member they belong?

Discuss the Book's Cover:
- How do the colors, shapes, illustrations on the cover make you feel? How might they be signaling belonging?

Vocabulary

Knapsack (n) a bag (often canvas or nylon) strapped on the back and used for carrying supplies or personal belongings

Ancestors (n) someone from whom a person is descended

Wobbling (adjective of "to wobble") to move or proceed with an irregular rocking or staggering motion or unsteadily and clumsily from side to side

Galaxies (n) (pl) any of the very large groups of stars and associated matter that are found throughout the universe

During Reading

- What does it mean to matter?
- Why is it important that everyone knows they matter?
- Turn and talk with a partner: How could you help someone else to feel that they matter?

Author's Craft:

- What do you notice about the illustrations? How do they make you feel? What details can you point out, and how might they relate to belonging?
- What does the author mean when she uses the simile, "...a book, like a mirror..."?

Interpretation:

- What sorts of feelings is the main character struggling with that cause him to question his place in the universe?
- How do you think the main character is reminded that he matters?

After Reading

- The author writes: "Did you know that you are sun rays, calm, like ocean waves, tough, like montañas, magic, like stars in space?" What makes you feel calm? Tough? Magical?
- What aspects of your history, family, community, or place of belonging do you feel pride in?
- Share some of your favorite affirmations and reminders (e.g., I am kind, I love my skin, I am a loyal friend). Read these aloud on days when you "question your place in the universe."
- Share "a book, like a mirror" books that you have read; post an ongoing list of books that feel like mirrors to individual students.

▶ For other favorite books on belonging, see page 200.

Belonging in Action

- Have students work together to create end-of-unit slideshows and short films that celebrate reading, using books on the belonging list, or create films that represent belonging to a club, a family, or the natural world.
- Have students work together on social media to create hashtag campaigns that promote belonging themes that are connected to the books you read.
- Share favorite belonging books online.
- Gather ideas for new books to read that will cultivate a discussion around belonging (e.g., anti-bullying, groups students belong to).
- Create a class document for students to share their ideas, reflections, and comments about the books they are reading and the books you are reading to them.

What You Can Do to Promote Belonging at Home

The first and most important thing we can do to create a sense of belonging in super reading at home is to be very clear with our families that we appreciate and honor their diverse learning experiences and styles, too. We can share podcasts and videos of ourselves and our students reading together for families to share at home (no matter what their own reading skills are). We can text message or communicate virtually in any way our school prefers to share the small moments of growth their children are having as readers, to model for them that it is not always about the big leap but also about these small moments, from decoding a hard word, to finishing one's first chapter book.

We can help mothers, fathers, grandparents, older siblings, and caregivers to feel a sense of belonging to reading that we do in school and also help them embrace the child into a community of readers at home. We can support families in how best to ask students to describe the day's work and listen and give practical tips for all families to encourage students to explore their emerging reader identities.

Let's encourage families to think of reading as a "together" activity to foster that sense of belonging. Adults and children can read different texts side by side, read multiple copies of the same book independently, or share a book. We recognize that not all adults in families will feel comfortable reading aloud if their own reading skills do not feel strong. We can support all families by encouraging reading aloud through pictures in picture books, or by sending home specific questions that can help lead to discussion of the pictures and the big themes in texts students are reading so that all families can enjoy books together, no matter their reading skills.

We often praise students who are star athletes. We line courts and fields each weekend, encouraging them. There's no mistaking whose kid just scored a goal; you only need to listen for the loudest, proudest voices! And those students are also beaming, not only because of their individual successes, but in seeing how proud and happy they have made their families. Imagine what it would do for students' reading lives if they were honored and praised for their reading in the same way. Create spaces for students to share their writing so that their families can celebrate the effort just as they would a virtuoso piano performance or a game-winning three-point shot.

Actions to Develop Children's Sense of Belonging at Home

Here are some activities for your students to do at home with their families. Select the ones you feel families would enjoy and which would develop students' sense of belonging most. You can reference them in emails to families or in your class newsletter.

 Book Baskets Create book baskets or online files for each family member that reflect the passions and interests of each person, honoring every member as a cherished person in this family unit.

 Heart Maps Have each family member draw a heart on a sheet of paper or on the computer and then fill it with words and images that represent where he or she has felt a deep sense of belonging.

 Family Interviews Have children interview family members about groups and communities to which they belong. They can ask questions like:

- Who is your best friend and why?
- What is your favorite thing to do?
- What was your favorite thing to do when you were my age?
- What group has felt important to you in your life?
- Where did you feel the greatest sense of belonging as a child?

 Family Mural Create a mural together with images that represent each member of the family.

 Family Favorites Book As a family, compile a list of favorite things to do together. Talk about your favorite things using prompts, including:

- What is your favorite book to read aloud?
- What is your favorite song to dance to together?
- Decorate your book with images and mementos, and keep it in a place of honor!

Routines to Develop Children's Sense of Belonging

- Create read-aloud times that are rituals, and make sure every family member gets a chance to select the reading.
- Talk about favorite and current reading material, from cereal boxes to novels.
- Choose books to read as a whole family.
- Create a listening corner for books online or on tape so multiple generations can listen together.
- Create book baskets or online files labeled with children's names and add to those baskets/files whenever students develop new interests (soccer, for example, and then add soccer books).
- Notice and celebrate unique qualities of children as readers. (Sarah loves animal books. Carlos reads books aloud to his little brother.)
- Share children's reading growth with grandparents.
- Encourage siblings to read together.
- Have children read to a pet or a stuffed animal!
- Host reading celebrations at home (tea and cake, etc.).
- Affirm and praise small steps in children's reading progress.
- Post reading accomplishments on the refrigerator or wall for all to see, or in a shared file to share with the extended family.

CHAPTER 4

STRENGTH TWO: FRIENDSHIP

"Let there be no purpose in friendship save the deepening of the spirit."

—KAHLIL GIBRAN

Roberto is an English language newcomer, having recently arrived to the United States from Nepal. Reading in English feels hard for him. Santina is a fluent reader. She is from Jordan. She reads from morning until night. They are both 10 years old. Their teacher has paired them as reading partners for the week. They are studying the theme of bullying in their whole-class discussions. In their reading partnership, Roberto is reading a book called *Addy's Cup of Sugar* by Jon J Muth. Santina is reading R. J. Palacio's *Wonder.* One is a picture book, and one is a chapter book. But Roberto and Santina can connect around the big themes of both books and back to the conversation of the whole class. At the end of the week, Roberto said to Santina, "You are a great reading friend to me." And Santina said, "I feel the same for you." Across levels, interests, across cultures, across languages, the shared, strengths-based themes bring them together and it is interesting to them to talk about the way the struggles of feeling ashamed or feeling lonely transcend cultures. They are united as super-reader friends.

Maria and Iliana came from Mexico to a large elementary school in Los Angeles within a month of each other—after the school year had started. Both brought strong language skills in Spanish and had received an excellent education in their home country. Fortunately, the third-grade class they joined included 12 children who spoke Spanish and English at home, two who spoke Vietnamese, and four who spoke solely English. The majority of the children understood the benefits and beauty of being a dual-language learner and knew that their home language was welcomed in the class. While listening to the teacher read aloud *In My Family/En Mi Familia* (Garza, 1996), which includes vignettes in both English and Spanish, one of the children suggested making a class book to add to the others in the library. Each child could write a vignette about their special family traditions and create a watercolor to support their writing, similar to the author's style. One student explained to Maria and Iliana, in Spanish, what the class would be creating and the joy on the girls' faces was unforgettable. Throughout the process, Maria and Iliana worked closely with their classmates to create their vignettes and artwork. When it was time for each student to share their writing during Author's Chair, several chose to share in both Spanish and English. Maria and Iliana shared in Spanish and received the same applause as their peers. For the teacher, it was a profound moment when she witnessed the power of literature to bring students together and the role that reading and writing could play in developing and solidifying friendships.

Elizabeth and Gregorio are editing short films on "youth voice" that the kids have created to share with wider audiences. Over the past four weeks they have been reading literature and talking with their peers about what it means for young people to play a powerful and positive role in social change. Although they are very young, Elizabeth already has the reputation of being a great filmmaker. "Lizzy, Lizzy," you can hear throughout the room as other kids want Lizzy's advice on their final editorial decisions. The films are due to be shown the next day! Gregorio doesn't call out to Lizzy. Instead he looks at the iMovie clips on his laptop with his head in his hands. He is at the breaking point, and there is no doubt he is considering an early retirement from the filmmaking profession. But Lizzy sees him and walks across the room and begins to speak to him in reassuring whispers. The expression on Gregorio's face changes as Lizzy reassures him that his film will be fine (which it is!). As she returns to her seat and puts her headphones back on to edit her own film, Lizzy is beaming. Her teacher gives her the subtle thumbs-up, and she nods like, "I know. I'm the champ." The next day all of the kids' short films are shown to great acclaim, including Gregorio's. Lizzy's film becomes a brief Internet sensation receiving thousands of views on Facebook and YouTube.

Why the Strength of Friendship Matters

We have seen from these past years, when our country and our world had to enter periods of isolation, how extraordinarily profound the importance of friendship is to all of us. We have shown in these examples all the ways young people can forge friendships even at a distance but how not being together in the daily messiness of life is an aching challenge. In the strengths-based classroom, friendship is a central element to not only how we learn to be good people in the world, but also how we learn to read and write. We are inspired by each other. We take care of each other. In the Super Reader Classroom, these are all values we cherish. But friendship takes work. It is a lifelong work in progress. And it is well worthwhile to show our students how we work on this art of friendship all our lives. We can be grateful and proud when we have a good friend. Books and stories teach us about friendship, too. Once again, the 7 Strengths are reciprocal—we practice friendship as active readers, and we also find friendship in the pages of the books we read together. Authors for all ages explore this journey and illuminate for us how those bumps in the road can translate to meaning and deepening of our lives in concert with one another.

In the strengths-based classroom, friendship is a central element to not only how we learn to be good people in the world, but also how we learn to read and write.

Educational psychologist Robert Selman has devoted much of his career to understanding friendship and its importance to students' health and well-being. Selman's Five Stages of Friendship Development are described in his 2007 book, *The Promotion of Social Awareness: Powerful Lessons From the Partnership of Developmental Theory and Classroom Practice*. Selman believes that the essence of friendship development is perspective taking, or the ability of young people to take into consideration other people's points of view. As the Yale Center for Emotional Intelligence founder Mark Brackett notes, "But the highest and most important analysis we conduct as we read is empathy. Before parsing out the significance of setting, before delving into the imagery, metaphors, symbols, and motifs, we must perform a critical analysis by which we open ourselves to the lives, feelings, and experiences of others. National Council of Teachers of English (NCTE) Ambassador Lindsay Schneider writes, "[t]hrough critical thinking, writing, reading, and rereading, we analyze texts and authors' craft in order to both gain empathy for lives we have not lived and for experiences we have not had, all while meeting a new character whom we come to care for deeply." (Schneider, 2020) Over time, as students learn to see those points of view and integrate them with their own, they are better able to manage relationships in their lives. A 2015 report from American Enterprise Institute and Brookings Institution tells us that fostering social competence is "critically important for the long-term success of all students in today's economy." In order to promote a vibrant community of learners, of super readers, in the classroom, in the home, or in the world, students need to learn the skill of perspective taking, and they need to be given plenty of opportunities in class and at home to practice that skill.

What You Can Do to Promote Friendship in Your Classroom

 Use literature to recognize the power, work, and complexities of friendship.

The power and magnificence of friendship courses its way through the greatest literature of our times, both classic and contemporary. Across cultures, languages, customs, and traditions, friendship's lasting value to society is clear. What we have not always recognized in the classroom, however, is how powerful it can be to academic development.

A first grader who reads Charlotte Agell's *Maybe Tomorrow?* learns about the gentle, life-affirming purpose of friendship. A third grader who reads *The Stories Julian Tells* discusses the tender and evocative moments of connection. The fifth grader who reads Kelly Yang's *Front Desk* for book club is moved to find that friendship can be complex and meaningful. The middle schooler can disappear into the Hunger Games series, finding that boys and girls can have friendships that may be more layered than they could have imagined.

Books such as those are guides, explorations, and exhilarations, helping students to navigate the most important connections of humanity. It is also interesting to study cultural similarities and differences about friendship, in spite of poverty, deep challenges, and separations. Your library collection should promote discussions, values, and inquiry related to friendship. Study good friendships in books as well as bumpy ones, for the bumpy ones can teach students how to be better friends and how to navigate hard situations with mutual respect and positive feelings. Create opportunities for students to label online folders and baskets for books in hand that bring texture to the study of friendship for them, too, and that they can talk about with partners, such as:

- friendships that last a long time
- friendships that face trouble
- friendships that are complicated
- friendships that are comforting/inspiring
- friendship role models/heroes

Work collaboratively to grow ideas.

People rely on one another to overcome obstacles and challenges, and friendship is so much a part of that. When Pam's father was sick in the hospital, she received a text from her friend Elizabeth: "I've come to the hospital. I know it's late, so I am going to be here in my car outside waiting, in case you should need me." In our classrooms, when students are working through big ideas, the hard work of reading, or seeking to write something, we must seize opportunities to celebrate, affirm, and cultivate collaboration that comes from trusting friendships. Friendship is life-giving, life-changing, and sometimes even lifesaving. It cannot be underestimated. We can use literature and also the example of making friends to learn together to give our children a lifetime resource for health and well-being.

Compare the friendships in stories you read to the work of the classroom. Use the friendship role models you find in texts to inform your teaching of classroom values. We saw how Elba and Norris supported each other in *Maybe Tomorrow?* We saw how Vicki Fang's characters always support each other while they are solving problems for others. How can we do the same while supporting our friends as they work through hard problems or difficult moments as readers or writers? Here are some practical ways to form friendship-driven partnerships among super readers in the classroom:

- Show students how to be careful, deep supporters of each other's work by providing concrete language: "I admire the way you worked through the hard part of that story." "I liked the idea you had about that problem."

- Create weekly partnerships that are formed based on things other than reading levels; perhaps similar questions students have about what they are reading, or similar interests in genre or writing type, or around passion for certain topics.

- Set up "Friendship Quests" where you encourage students to pair up with a "new" friend in the class, someone they do not know as well, and have them do a fun problem together, write a story together, or listen online to a story and record each other in a mini-interview talking about the book.

- In shared online documents and blogs, have students coauthor responses to texts and ideas they've been building. There are students who will prefer to nurture friendships in writing or by exchanging snippets of audio or video. In the "old" days, these students would have been considered shy. But today, those same students have the chance to have active, "talkative" lives of learning and collaboration with the support of online technologies.

Build a powerful community through friendship.

We can cultivate friendships through active forms of literacy, such as singing, reciting poetry, engaging in group projects, participating in collective writing projects, journaling to one another, establishing e-pals, and celebrating/respecting other opinions about texts. Reader and writer's theater, bringing to life picture books, chapter books, poetry, and even informational texts, can bring out students' inner lives, stories, and strengths, lifting academics up off the page and into the spirit of community. Illuminate the fact that you will celebrate a child who reaches out to another child for friendship. Admire the super reader who initiates:

- A Friendship Lunch—bringing a lunch for a friend and a book to share.

- A book exchange at holiday time.

- A special section of the classroom library called "Recommended by a Friend."

- Friend Chats About Books, which can happen any time of day, from recess to the minutes after students arrive at school. Keep cards or sticky notes handy, or if you are doing this online, a special place for recording what the chat was about.

FRIENDSHIP FOCUS LESSON

Friendship Chain

By analyzing their own experiences with friendly relationships and those of characters in books, super readers can be encouraged to reflect on the importance of friendship to their community.

Directions

1. Introduce the lesson by saying:

   The strong relationships we have with others have so much power in our lives. There are gentle, tender things friends do to make people feel happy and create a sense of well-being. Let's reflect on this today as we create Friendship Chains. This thinking will help us explore ways we can become good friends to each other.

2. Explain to students they will write an action of a good friend on one side of a paper strip—for example: "Friends stand up for you." On the other side, have them write the name of a real person or a fictional character they know who has carried out that action. You can say:

   Let's take a few minutes to brainstorm some of the things good friends do. For example: friends stand up for you, friends cheer you up when you're feeling down. You're going to record one of these actions. On the back of the strip, you can record the names of people you know or characters you have read about who have acted in this way! For example, you could write, "Friends help each other be brave." You can write about characters who have been stand-up friends, or describe ways you want to be a friend in the world.

3. Encourage students to write and draw. Encourage them to be specific in the actions they identify.

4. Once students have created their strips, ask them to staple them into links to create a chain that can be displayed or taken home.

5. Have students share some of the actions they wrote down and discuss some of the most common ones. Connect these actions to students' interactions within their reading community. Ask them, "How can practicing ways to be a good friend help us make our reading community stronger?"

Actions to Promote Friendship in the Super Reader Classroom

Friendship Collage	Have students create a collage celebrating powerful elements of friendship with different kinds of images (a lion photo, for example, to demonstrate fierce loyalty).
Friendship Memory Book	Invite students to create a friendship book where they collect their favorite memories of their friends during the school year.
Friendship Bill of Rights	Invite students to draft a list of 10 qualities they strive to have as a good friend.
Bookmark Buddies	Ask students to create their own bookmarks by drawing an image of a book character they believe would be a good friend in real life. Encourage them to use the bookmarks and take the characters on their upcoming journeys through new books.
Friendship Circle	Create opportunities for Circle Time (at any age), virtually or in person, to honor some small or big way someone in the community has given grace to another, stepping toward a friendship goal, or reached out to someone new.

INTERACTIVE READING LESSON

Maybe Tomorrow?

by Charlotte Agell
illustrated by Ana Ramírez González

FRIENDSHIP

Summary: In *Maybe Tomorrow?* by Charlotte Agell, Elba's heart is heavy as she goes through each day struggling to find optimism. One day, an unexpected friendship with Norris opens up a new world of hope and teaches Elba the power of having a true friend.

Before Reading

Discuss Friendship:
- What feels most important to you about friendship?
- What are one or two of the most important things friends can do to support one another?

Vocabulary

Shininess (n of adjective "shiny") having a smooth, glossy surface

Prodding (v) to thrust a pointed instrument into

Whisper (v) to speak softly with little or no vibration of the vocal cords, especially to avoid being overheard

Flitted (v) to pass quickly or abruptly from one place or condition to another

Damp (adj) moisture; humidity; wetness

Horizon (n) the line where the earth or sea seems to meet the sky

During Reading

Interpretation:
- What kind of friend might Norris be and can you share evidence of that?
- Why do you think Elba's block had shrunk by the time they made it to the beach?

"I miss Little Bird," said Elba
as they crested the last hill.
"She is gone."

"I miss her, too," said Norris.
Elba paused.
"But you didn't know her."
"No, but you are my friend,
so I can help you miss her."

Author's Craft:
- What does this illustration inspire in you about friendship?
- How do the author's descriptive words add to the story? Can you find any?

After Reading
- What do Norris and Elba teach us about friendship?
- What type of feelings do you think Elba's block is made of? How about Norris' butterflies?
- Why are Norris and Elba good friends?
- How can you be a good friend? In what ways is friendship important in your life?

▶ For other favorite books on friendship, see pages 200–201.

Friendship in Action

- Help students craft online messages to friends and family members about their favorite books.
- Let students connect online with friends and family members to share what they are reading. Encourage a child to develop a digital-pal relationship with a friend or family member who lives far away to talk about the books that they like.
- Look for ways for students to find like-minded friends who love similar types of texts.
- Arrange for students to be digital pals with a classroom in a different community or country. Use face-to-face digital communication tools to facilitate conversations.

What You Can Do to Promote Friendship at Home

The type of work you do in promoting relationship building and budding friendships at school can be done by families at home, too. The home and the community are ideal places to teach students the value and work of friendship and to begin to connect friendship to becoming super readers.

Encourage families to choose books to read with their children that highlight friendship. Stress the importance of talking productively with their children about what it means to be a good friend. You can help families model friendship by sharing sentence starters with them about the characteristics of good friendship like empathy, concern, being a good listener, or showing support. Provide questions such as the following:

- When have you felt like a good friend?
- When has being a friend felt hard?
- What are the qualities of good friends?
- How can characters in books we've read or you've read help you forge a path to friendship?

- How can I help you mend a friendship?
- Sometimes friendships aren't always so good for us. How can we be more honest with each other when something is not working?

Families can also form family or neighborhood book or storytelling clubs that encourage friendships around reading and sharing great books. With digital technologies, kids and families can create virtual book chats with distant relatives and friends in other parts of the world. This takes some planning, so consider giving families specific instructions or assignments that will encourage those activities.

Actions to Develop Children's Sense of Friendship at Home

Here are some activities for your students to do at home with their families. Select the ones you feel families would enjoy and that would develop students' sense of belonging most. You can reference them in emails to families or in your class newsletter.

	Friendship Collage	Create a collage where children identify meaningful friendship traits in their family members and friends.
	Friendship Memory Book	Invite children to create a friendship book where they collect favorite memories with family members and friends.
	Family and Friends Dinner	Encourage families to organize a dinner where each person invites a friend and reads aloud together.
	Friendship Chain	Cut pieces of paper into strips. Family members can record a way they are a good friend, and a way others are good friends to them. They can then link the strips by taping or stapling the ends together to make a Friendship Chain to hang in the home.
	Friendship Circle	At dinner or anytime when the family has a quiet moment together, share one way big or small that someone in the family has expressed friendship to another person, inside or outside the family, and set friendship goals for the coming week.

Routines to Develop Children's Sense of Friendship

- Read books around the theme of friendship.
- Model reading behaviors for book clubs or with book buddies.
- Ask children to share their favorite books.

CHAPTER 5

STRENGTH THREE: KINDNESS

"We carry with us, as human beings, not just the capacity to be kind, but the very choice of kindness."

—R.J. PALACIO

Like clockwork, at 10:30 each morning, Matthew would open the door to the third-grade classroom, look around, and cautiously step inside. He towered over most of the students, at least by a foot, and was shy and quiet. Initially, he was embarrassed to come to the class as a fourth grader, but his special education teacher and the third-grade teacher thought he would thrive in a class doing math at his level with a hands-on, project-based learning approach. And like clockwork, the teacher would smile and the room would erupt with enthusiastic phrases including "Hi, Matthew!" "Here's a seat!" and "Come sit with us today!" The daily ritual took about 30 seconds from the time he stepped into the room until he found a seat. However, the overwhelming impact of so many positive words and genuine kindness could not be measured. Did Matthew grow as a mathematician that year? By leaps and bounds. He knew he was welcomed, he knew we cared about him, and small words and acts of kindness blossomed into friendships at recess and in the classroom.

Marisol, age 10, wrote in her notebook that, because of her time in foster care, she had never had a birthday party. She wrote about what she'd wish for at a party if she had one—a big beautiful white cream cake with pink frosting, a music playlist with all her favorite mariachi songs, and yellow and orange and pink balloons. She read this story aloud to her class, and soon after, members of the class approached us. "We'd like to make Marisol the birthday party she never had," they told us. And so, they and their families took action. They decorated the room with yellow and orange and pink balloons. They made a cake, white cream of course, with pink frosting. They created a playlist with all her favorite songs. Marisol and her friends danced and sang. The act of kindness shown by her classmates drew from her own story and from the kind of environment that valued the telling and sharing of personal stories. Kindness is an act of social justice. Students can learn in everyday ways how personal stories can fuel the power of kindness and how kindness can change the world. Marisol was touched by the kindness of her friends, but her friends were also touched by Marisol's story. And Marisol got to tell a new story after that day, a story emblematic of the 7 Strengths classroom, where reading one's own stories and writing down one's own life makes a difference.

Why Kindness Matters

Kindness stays with us for a lifetime. Our students will remember and be influenced by that positive energy, and within a strengths-based classroom they can practice kindness, too. We have seen over and over again in our work that when the classroom feels like a safe space for kindness to flourish, so much learning also flourishes. When LitCamp began to spread across the country, over and over we heard that not only were students excelling in literacy, there was literally no trace of bullying or marginalization, as there had been with the very same kids in the past. The culture of the strengths is a shield, a protector, and a pathway to a new kind of community.

The major inhibitors of learning—stress, abuse, trauma—can be all too present in a child's early years. Research out of Harvard University's Center on the Developing Child shows that though a child's temperament and early experiences may affect his or her learning initially, the cumulative impact of positive experiences make it easier for him or her to achieve positive outcomes (National Scientific Council on the Developing Child, 2015). Programs that incorporate meaningful connections between staff and students, as well as between student and student, contribute significantly to this development of resilience. The founder and director of Yale's Center for Emotional Intelligence explains, "[a]lthough our students will never have lives free of hardship and troubling events, we can help them have lives full of healthy relationships, compassion, and a sense of purpose—by teaching them to work with their emotions." (Brackett, 2018)

Nel Noddings observes in her book *Happiness and Education* (2003) that children and adults alike learn best when they are happy, while sustained stress can physically alter the neural connections of the brain. Creating a positive learning environment for students can combat traumatic or detrimental experiences such as child abuse, poverty, malnourishment, or family and community violence that may hinder their learning. As Nodding states, "Brain research reveals superior learning takes place when classroom experiences are relevant to students' lives, interests, and experiences."

Cultivating supportive relationships within the classroom is the first step to fostering super readers who will impact the world beyond it. One key ingredient to creating these types of spaces is kindness. When adults and peers model and encourage kindness, students come to appreciate how it feels to be treated with kindness and the joy that comes from extending kindness to others.

What You Can Do to Promote Kindness in Your Classroom

Value tenderness.

There are many ways a reading community can value tenderness. First, be sure there are examples of tenderness in the texts you are reading—in picture books, chapter books, informational texts, and poems. In the picture book *Stevie* by John Steptoe, two characters find ways to express kindness for each other, even though one at first feels supplanted by the other. Through informational texts, students can learn about kindness. In *Koko's Kitten*, for example, the author shares a special bond between a large gorilla and a kitten. In *14 Cows for America*, Carmen Agra Deedy shows the breathtaking way a small African village makes an enormous impact with a very special gift following the events of September 11th.

Studying point of view in literature can have a far-reaching influence on a child's ability to respect perspectives that may be different from his or her own. When we give students opportunities through literature to witness the other side of a story or the internal struggle of a beloved character, we arm them with knowledge about the complexities of our social world. The more students experience a love of character, the more they develop the muscle to love one another—and become super readers.

In the classroom, value tenderness by showing you care about it. Create a Kindness Box to which students can add a note whenever they spot an act of kindness. Throw a celebration when the box is full. Have a Kindness Hero of the Week; celebrate characters in books who demonstrate kindness. In *Leadership: The Power of Emotional Intelligence*, Daniel Goleman stresses the importance of having leaders who can demonstrate cognitive and emotional empathy. He explains: "Because you understand other perspectives, you can put things in ways colleagues comprehend. And you welcome their questions, just to be sure. Cognitive empathy, along with reading another person's feelings accurately, makes for effective communication." In other words, kindness and tenderness are not "soft skills." They are crucial to creating future leaders, as well as super readers.

Make time for affirmation.

Recognize acts of kindness. Make role models of students who exhibit empathy regularly. However, be aware that often those students are the ones who are not noticed—they are the ones who let everyone else "go first," give things away, don't compete with others, and are not the first to raise their hands. It often takes an astute teacher to notice and value empathy. Make public compliments that affirm those students:

- Thank you, John, for making it possible for Sarah to speak first.

- I want to appreciate Gabriella and Jeremy for demonstrating strong and caring partnership skills today.

- I saw that Emily was challenged by a hard word and that Hakim took the lead in supporting her, and I want to compliment them on working together.

Explore the role of kindness as an interpersonal asset.

One child reading to another child is in its own way a powerful act of kindness. Organize cross-grade-level partner read-alouds for World Read Aloud Day, the first Wednesday in February each year. Reach across cultural divides by sharing read alouds with partner schools through video conference calls or Internet chats.

Partnerships like those are beautiful ways to help students practice kindness; it is how they become strong partners, how they learn to be supportive and kind speakers and listeners who pause intentionally and value the small moves people make when they are affirming one another. Praise is so easy to offer and often so easily overlooked. Help students by setting the stage for a life of kindness.

Offer language that super readers can use with one another, such as:

- What I think you are saying is...
- I really admire the hard work you did today as a reader.
- I enjoyed working with you today.
- I'd like to help you...
- How can I be of support?

When we are kind, we take people seriously, no matter their age. We need to teach students the skills of active speaking and listening and help them build definitions of what a culture of kindness means to them by modeling our own abundant kindness and care. In this way, they go home and do the very same for their loved ones. Many times, we have heard parents say that students go home and "play" LitCamp and that when they do, the mainframe of how they play is how they help each other and take good care of each other. Isn't this super reader world the world we all dream of and long for?

KINDNESS FOCUS LESSON

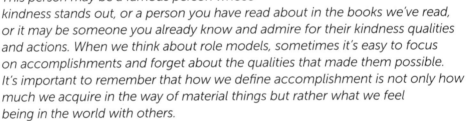

Kindness Heroes

By guiding super readers to celebrate kindness in people and characters they admire, you can encourage them to reflect on the importance of this strength to members of a reading community.

Directions

1. Introduce the lesson by saying:

   Today we are going to discuss Kindness Heroes. This person may be a famous person whose kindness stands out, or a person you have read about in the books we've read, or it may be someone you already know and admire for their kindness qualities and actions. When we think about role models, sometimes it's easy to focus on accomplishments and forget about the qualities that made them possible. It's important to remember that how we define accomplishment is not only how much we acquire in the way of material things but rather what we feel being in the world with others.

2. Ask students to think about some of the people they look up to. You can say:

   For a few minutes, let's all think about people we look up to. This can be a real person, someone from history, or a character in a book. Let's choose someone whose kindness played a big role in his or her life and success.

3. Offer some examples to help clarify this for students. You can say:

   Let's talk about some examples of people who exemplify kindness: Malala Yousafzai is a Kindness Role Model. She is a Pakistani girl who stood up for the right of all girls to get an education. Even after the Taliban attacked her, she continued to stand up for what she believed in. Malala demonstrates kindness and compassion every day as she champions girls around the world.

4. After discussing these examples, give the students time to think of their own Kindness Role Models and write about why kindness was important to their success. Tell them they don't need to write a lot, just two or three sentences, or they can draw or sketch.

5. Once each student has chosen a figure and written or drawn a little bit about him or her, share whatever material you think feels good, either online or offline, to create posters. You can say:

Now we will create posters to celebrate our Kindness Role Models. Let's each draw an image of a person we admire. Create art and/or words around this person and their inspiration to you.

6. Be sure to leave a few minutes for sharing student work and discussing the activity, and praise everyone for creating their posters and sharing their ideas. Guiding questions might include:

   - Did you learn about any new kindness role models today? What is one that inspired you, and why?

   - Why might kindness be necessary as we read and learn together? Name specific situations where kindness would be important.

   - When does kindness feel hard? Why?

   - How can we help each other remember to be kind? How can we be kind to ourselves?

7. As an extension activity, have students write or draw a kindness commitment they want to make to themselves or others around them. They can share these orally or via technology, or write or draw them to post in the room.

8. As a homework extension activity, encourage families to research the child's Kindness Role Model together. Ask adults and children at home to share who their Kindness Role Models are.

Actions to Promote Kindness in School and in the Super Reader Classroom

Kindness Webs	Create webs based on the books you read. Have students give each character his or her own circle, and then draw lines to connect the characters who have been kind to each other. Students can write a description of each kind act along the lines.
Kindness in Action	Create a running list of kindness actions you see others doing, from the children to the adults in the school, that you can add to continually and emulate where possible.
Kindness Hall of Fame	Look for examples of kindness in books read together and post them on a Kindness Hall of Fame.
Messages of Kindness	Invite everyone to write kind, anonymous messages to students in the class that you distribute.

INTERACTIVE READING LESSON

Addy's Cup of Sugar

by Jon J Muth
illustrated by Jon J Muth

Summary: In *Addy's Cup of Sugar* by Jon J Muth, Addy is grieving after the loss of her beloved pet cat and seeks the help of her friend Stillwater the panda for a solution. Addy learns lessons about her neighbors and herself in a journey to find the medicine for a broken heart.

Before Reading	**Discuss Kindness:** • What does *kindness* mean to you? Why is it important to be kind to both people you know and those you don't? • Why might kindness be important in times of grief and sadness?
During Reading	**Interpretation**: • Why couldn't Addy find anyone from whom to borrow sugar? • What does Addy mean on this page when she says, "The medicine was for me, wasn't it?"

Vocabulary

Ingredients (n) things that are component parts of any combination or mixture

Medicine (n) a substance or preparation used in treating disease

Scampered (v) to run nimbly and usually playfully about

Curled (v) to form into a curved shape

"But I understand now," she said.
"The medicine was for me, wasn't it?"

Stillwater smiled a beautiful sad smile.

Author's Craft:
- How does the author tell us about Trumpet and Addy through characterization?
- Why do you think the author decided to break up the text on this page in this way? How does that influence the way we read it?

She thought of Trumpet. Of how he chased dragonflies in the yard. How she would find him curled up asleep in the funniest places. How his little pink toes felt so soft. How he would purr and rub his chin against her cheek while she lay in the grass looking at the clouds.

Now she felt the tears come.

Interpretation:
- Choose a page with a partner and see if you can both decipher from Addy's expression what she is feeling and why.

After Reading
- How does her neighbor's kindness help Addy to feel less alone?
- What does Addy learn about missing someone you care about?
- What does Addy's trip around her neighborhood teach us about the importance of being kind, even to those we don't know much about?

▶ For other favorite books on kindness, see page 202.

Kindness in Action

- Have students use cameras to capture images of kindness in class, the community, and at home. Assemble the images in a slideshow that can be shared with others.
- Ask students to identify and take on the perspective of kind characters from their favorite books and stories.
- Locate organizations focused on promoting kindness in the community and the world, and find ways to support them.
- Have students create a blog or a website on a social issue and how they can respond with kindness actions, or share ideas with each other that they are learning from literature that will promote kindness (anti-bullying action steps, for example).

What You Can Do to Promote Kindness at Home

You can help your families use reading, writing, and discussion to think about and plan ways they can use kindness to affect the world around them.

Encourage families to provide opportunities for students to see themselves demonstrating kindness in the home, in the community, and in the larger world. An older sibling can become a reading buddy with a younger brother or sister. Students may use technology to become reading buddies with a distant aunt, uncle, or grandparent. Perhaps families can volunteer to do community service together such as reading to sight-impaired residents of a nursing home, writing letters to soldiers, or tutoring at the library.

Suggest that families host kindness conversations. Families can talk with children about social problems that they see in their community and in the larger society, and they can discuss as a family what they might do to help solve those problems. Remind families to listen to their children in these conversations and to honor the opinions and perspectives they bring to the discussions.

Encourage families to find innovative ways to measure and reward acts of kindness in the home and in the community. Families can model kindness in everyday social interactions, and they can help students understand that kindness is more than being nice; it is also a genuine concern for others and a way of using reading, writing, listening, and speaking to improve the world in some way. Some of the best examples of kindness are those closest to home. Suggest to families that when a child kisses a baby sibling goodnight or helps his or her grandmother to bring the food to the table, these are kindness moments. You might even consider sending home kindness star stickers for families to use when they "catch" a child in an act of quiet kindness.

Actions to Develop Children's Sense of Kindness at Home

Here are some activities for your students to do at home with their families. Select the ones you feel families would enjoy and which would develop students' sense of kindness most. You can reference them in emails to families or in your class newsletter.

	Kindness Webs	Create webs based on the books you read. Give each character his or her own circle, and then draw lines to connect the characters who have been kind to each other. Write a description of each kind act along the lines.
	Kindness in Action	Create a running list of kindness actions that children can add to continually, and take action on one each week.
	Kindness Hall of Fame	Look for examples of kindness in books you and children read together and post them on a Kindness Hall of Fame.
	Messages of Kindness	Invite family members to write, text, or record messages of kindness to send to extended family members near and far.
	I Am Kind	Have everyone choose one small way to demonstrate kindness to the rest of the family and commit to doing it!

Routines to Develop Children's Sense of Kindness

- Let children know when someone showed you kindness and how it made you feel.

- Help children keep track of acts of kindness they have received.

- Encourage children to do an act of kindness each day, and then post a "kindness star" on the refrigerator with children's good deeds written on it.

- Talk about digital citizenship. What does it feel like when someone is being kind to you online? When have you expressed kindness online?

- Create ways to reach out to your local community, even virtually, to offer a helping hand. Then, as a family, keep a journal about your actions.

- Value and honor the language we use in the home around sharing and expressing ideas. Teach language like "I want to add on to what you are saying…" or "I hear your perspective and would like to offer another."

- Develop a philanthropy project with children inspired by a character in a book.

- Have children start a blog showing ways to be kind and promoting acts of kindness.

CHAPTER 6

STRENGTH FOUR: CURIOSITY

*"All books are imagination incubators.
They are spaces for kids to grow their imaginations,
work out problems, and ask: what does it mean
to do the right thing?"*

—SAYANTANI DASGUPTA

I n Los Angeles, a group of early adolescents are reading Rudolfo Anaya's *Bless Me, Ultima*, a novel that features a 12-year-old protagonist who is journeying between Mexico and the United States. As many of the students in the class are also recent immigrants from Mexico, they become interested in their own families' stories of immigration. The final project for the unit involves students conducting oral history interviews with two elders in their families. The students create short reports about these interviews that are accompanied by slide show presentations that they share with their classmates, family, and friends. Many of the students and their families comment that they learned things about themselves and their families that they would not have known were it not for the oral history assignment. The curiosity sparked by reading a story opened the opportunity for early adolescents to conduct their own research into their families and communities.

Young Fiona, age 6, is curious about nursing homes. Her grandpa, who has lived with the family since she was born, is now moving into one. In the Super Reader Classroom, she is encouraged to explore her curious questions, interview her grandfather and his friends, read and reread their responses, and write a "research" report on her perspective. She determined that "nursing homes are pretty good because Grandad and his friends like the Macaroni and Cheese Fridays!"

Why Curiosity Matters

Curiosity leads to invention and innovation. Many creative CEOs have prized curiosity in the workplace because it helps colleagues solve problems and work collaboratively (Gates, 2000). It is a strength that reaches across disciplines and is seen in the youngest child—the child who explores the world by asking "Why? Why? Why?"

Children are naturally hungry for information. Babies explore by touching and tasting, gazing with wide-eyed wonder at the world around them. As they get older, children question, which is a reflection of an ingrained need to always know more.

However, that curiosity, which is often so evident in a child's early life, is often suppressed when we value quiet obedience over active inquiry. In Susan Engel's classroom study, curiosity was measured by the number of questions asked in a two-hour period (Engel, 2015). While kindergartners asked two to five questions in this time frame, many fifth graders went a full day without showing any signs of inquisitiveness. The lack of questions in classrooms is a direct consequence of students' disengagement from reading, writing, and a love of learning. Without this critical engagement, we deprive students of their most powerful tool for achievement: their own insatiable appetites for knowledge.

Curiosity leads to invention and innovation. It is a strength that reaches across disciplines and is seen in the youngest child—the child who explores the world by asking "Why? Why? Why?"

Curiosity leads super readers to unknown territory, and they can't chart a new course without circling back a few times. They will not be able to be curious if they see failure as a negative. An article in the *Harvard Business Review* contends that, in a complex world, curiosity is as important as intelligence. (*Harvard Business Review*, 2014) It takes humility for people to consider information that contradicts their opinions. And it takes curiosity for people to actively seek evidence that challenges their views and to willingly concede that they might be wrong.

What You Can Do to Promote Curiosity in Your Classroom

Practice Wondering the "Five Whys."

Curiosity in the classroom blossoms when the community to which all students belong is healthy and supportive. There are many ways to encourage curiosity. The classroom is the ideal space to teach students to ask questions, to wonder, and to celebrate those behaviors when you spot them. In our classrooms, students should be encouraged to ask questions of text, of the world, and of each other. Wondering strategies might include "Ask Five Whys," in which we encourage students to ask five questions that begin with "Why" about a topic of interest. Make any wondering feel like a game: the deeper we dig, the more we discover. You can play this game with a book you are reading, or just in conversation with each other. Model the use of the word "wonderings" as it is an open-ended, friendly way of hearing other people's thoughts.

Embrace inquiry-based instruction.

To acquire language, learning through inquiry has emerged as a means that allows for smoother and more effective communication (Alameddine & Ahwal, 2016). You can have students actively involved in following a line of inquiry inspired by the books that they are reading. Identify driving questions for inquiry and share those questions with the students. (For example, a teacher asks the class, "What makes a person a hero?" and shares that she herself is not sure about the answer, and invites students to join her as they together uncover an answer.) Also, questions can be geared toward identifying a problem that needs solving, thereby launching a research and/or engineering cycle. ("Why do so many kids not finish their school lunch?"; "What can we build that will keep the deer away from our garden so our plants can thrive?")

Use literature to foster wonderings.

Through the read-aloud and interactive reading experiences, students can come to see literature as a springboard for their own deepest questions and wonderings. They can use literature as a launching point for independent research, or for turn-and-talk discussions with a partner. (See Chapter 10 for more information.) In modeling curiosity, ask open-ended questions that lead to lines of inquiry for you and your students.

Some of the prompts we can use to encourage engagement and curiosity around text include:

- Stop and jot a wondering you have right now about what you are reading.
- Why are you feeling moved by this text?
- Why do you think the author made that decision?
- What is your opinion/claim/hypothesis about (a character, plot, setting, idea, fact)?
- What are you curious to learn more about?
- What are you wondering about your own culture and language?
- How can you ask your family or community questions that would guide you to more knowledge?
- What are you wondering about other people who live in different places?
- How can we find out more about our wonderings?

In a first-grade class, students read the notes written by author Nic Bishop about how he uses primary sources as a way to drive and deepen his curiosity for the world. He writes: "I love to play science detective and dig my way down to the bedrock of scientific data published in the primary literature. As well as really being able to check up on the facts, written in the scientist's own words, I can sometimes find new things to use in my books." He revels in the joy of "sifting through the scientist's original tables and charts."

Use the world as a lens to build curiosity.

Affirm students' desire to marvel at ideas, whether they are gathered around a book, looking out the window, or exploring the outdoors together. Capture their curiosity by making book baskets (or bookmarks online) for their big topics of wondering. Have easily available informational texts, scientific journals, magazines, and picture books that reflect the passions of the students, from sports to collections to popular culture. More value should be placed on the questions students ask than on finding correct answers to teacher-created questions. Let us create safe environments in which to ask questions that we and the students don't know the answers to. Let us post our favorite wonderings and keep them up on the walls with boxes of index cards nearby so students can add on to their thinking as the year progresses to bigger questions that take longer to answer. ("How long would it take for a turtle to cross the United States?" "What kinds of family stories do the Navajo Nation tell?" "Who invented Disney movies, and how did they get made?")

Value the power of peer-to-peer interaction.

In the 7 Strengths classroom, student-to-student interaction should be valued in terms of asking questions—asking each other questions and sharing longer-term wonderings, as well as making plans for how to do research together to get wonderings answered.

How do students use literature? Books like *The Watsons Go to Birmingham—1963* by Christopher Paul Curtis, *Write to Me: Letters from Japanese American Children to the Librarian They Left Behind* by Cynthia Grady, and *Catching a Story Fish* by Janice N. Harrington might prompt students to think about society as a whole and the ways they can influence it. *The Life I'm In* by Sharon Flake may prompt curiosity about extending empathy to those who hurt us. In each new book, there is a new lesson about students' world and themselves.

Model great questioning by turning surface-level questions:

- "What is the author teaching us about?"

into questions that uncover a deeper meaning:

- "What is the deepest theme this author may be exploring?"

Post exemplary questions for discussing literary texts:

- "What might the illustration tell you about the character's feelings?"
- "What may be making the character change her mind?"
- "What lesson could we learn from what happened in the story?"

as well as informational texts:

- "Does the author appear to be objective or biased? Why?"
- "What words or phrases did the author use to try to persuade you?"
- "What do you think the author needed to do to prepare to write this piece?"

Encourage super readers to consider point of view:

- "What aspects of the text reveal the author's point of view or purpose?"
- "Why is it important to identify the points of view of others and how they are alike or different from our own?"

Curiosity Poems

By incorporating super readers' questions about the world into poems, you can encourage them to think deeply about topics that make them curious, and spark their desire to read to find out more.

Directions

1. Introduce the lesson by saying:

   As humans, we always have so many questions. Some are about how things work and why things happen. Some are about the human experiences we have and our emotions, while others are about the world around us. Today, we are going to turn our wonderings into poems and art.

2. Ask students to think about questions they might have about their world.
   You can say:

   Let's make a list or share with a partner some of the wonderings we have about ourselves, our communities, the world around us, or far away. Star one of those wonderings. For these poems, you can either explore one of these wonderings or write a poem of your many wonderings. It is up to you.

3. Invite each student to write a poem based on his or her question. You can say:

   Now we are going to turn our questions into poems! You can write any type of poem you like, rhyming or no rhyme, short or long! Any type of poem you come up with is great, as long as it asks a question about the thing you are interested in.

   If a student struggles to write a poem, suggest that he or she use the question as the first line of the poem, or as the title.

4. Have students decorate their work, set the poems to music online, or create video montages with the poems as background narration.

5. Have students do a "turn and talk" with a partner, and if online, share in complimentary ways.

6. Lead a discussion about the activity with students. Ask them questions such as:

   • How did it feel to write a poem about a topic you are curious about? Was it hard or easy? Why?

   • Did writing this poem spark any more questions for you about your topic?

   • Did you learn anything about one of your classmates or the topic of the poem after listening to his or her poem?

   • How can you find out more about your topic? (Encourage students to be specific. e.g., "a website about pandas" vs. "the Internet.")

7. Display students' poetry proudly! You can have a "Wondering Wall" where you celebrate the curiosity within all of your students.

8. As an extension activity, provide students the opportunity to seek answers to their questions in books and online.

Actions to Promote Curiosity in the Super Reader Classroom

Wonder Walk	Bring a tablet or notebook and teach students how to take notes on a walk to document wonderings and observations.
Book Club	Create a book club centered around topics that make students wonder.
Author Questions	Keep a running list of questions students would love to ask the authors of their favorite books.
Curiosity Tour	Have each child select a wondering they have and then explore together online or at the library, or by talking to experts around us for some responses to those wonderings.
Three Stories	Ask students to go around in a group and share three stories; two stories are true and one is untrue. The other students have to find out which story is untrue.
20 Questions	Play a game where one student stands in the center of a circle and selects someone to be like an animal or famous athlete. The student acts this out, and the rest of the group has to figure out what or who the student is by asking yes/no questions. If the group does that before 20 questions, they win the round.

INTERACTIVE READING LESSON

The Magician's Hat

by Malcolm Mitchell
Illustrated by Joanne Lew-Vriethoff

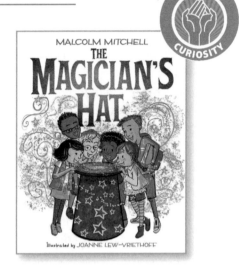

Summary: In *The Magician's Hat* by Malcolm Mitchell, a world of wonder appears to children who dare to dream of their futures. With the help of good books, some curiosity, and a sprinkle of magic, anything is possible.

Before Reading	**Discuss Curiosity:** • What do you wonder about? What big questions do you ask yourself? • What are you curious about in your reading life before you start a new book? **Discuss the Book's Cover:** • What do you think this book might be about? • What are you wondering about this book's title?

Vocabulary

Magician (n) one who performs tricks of illusion, or one who can do impossible things by saying special words or performing special actions

Vanished (v) to pass quickly from sight; to disappear

Dazzle (v) to impress deeply, overpower, or confound with brilliance

Snickered (v) to laugh in a secret or partly suppressed manner

During Reading

- Are the children in this story curious? How might you know?
- What are your wonderings about the first two pages of illustrations? What do you notice? What questions do you have?

- What does the author mean when he says a question can "[make] magic"?
- Discuss the purpose of dialogue in stories. With a partner, create a brief dialogue for the characters to continue talking.
- How do you think curiosity helped the children throughout the story?
- How do you think Ryan felt when he pulled out a book about space?

After Reading

- Have you ever been curious about your future? What do you wonder about?
- What type of book might you find in the magician's hat? What do you want to be when you grow up?
- How does curiosity play a role in your life?
- What does curiosity do to make your life more interesting?

▶ For other favorite books on curiosity, see pages 201–202.

Curiosity in Action

- Have students create a narrated slideshow with questions they have about a book.
- Create a class or family box or computer folder where students can store research projects and work on them collaboratively.
- Work with students to use online search tools to discover answers to questions. Have them refine their search queries to optimize their search results.
- Teach students how to use the online resources of public libraries and universities for their literature-related research.

What You Can Do to Promote Curiosity at Home

You have an important role in helping families encourage a healthy sense of curiosity in their children. Curiosity is really a process of inquiry, of constantly searching for answers. Let families know that this requires a tremendous amount of patience and openness to the child-centered idea but that you believe in their ability to do so. A home that hopes to cultivate curiosity will need to make that space an unstructured, unrestricted time for exploration. Such a home will celebrate the journey even more than the destination.

Encourage families to follow the child's interests and curiosities and expand upon them to build a world of information around the books they read. You might have them:

- Do an Internet search about the setting of a book.
- Use a smartphone to look up unfamiliar words or phrases.
- Build background of historical events or periods mentioned in the books they read by consulting informational articles or streaming videos.
- Travel to a destination mentioned in a book, or use the Internet to take a virtual tour.
- Keep a wall of wonderings.

Request that families allow time for children's uninterrupted exploration and that they encourage and celebrate a sense of wonder. Provide families with tips about the types of tools (book bins, magazines, technology) and activities (free browsing, making collages, playing literature-based games) to make available to children to encourage this type of inquiry.

When homework is given, select assignments that promote literacy-based inquiry, such as a family research project. Encourage families to participate in meaningful discussions at home during which they encourage children to ask open-ended questions of the world and to follow up on those questions. Get families outside when possible to explore nature and to use that curiosity as a launching point for reading and writing. Create home and community scavenger hunts that connect to the books that you read. Finally, remind families that they can be role models of curious learners, lifelong explorers, and critical questioners of the world by asking open-ended questions with their children.

Curiosity lends itself to all kinds of exploration, so this is a good time to bring family "experts" to the classroom. From the mom who is a nurse practitioner to the dad who is an electrician, they can be invited in to talk about how their curiosity leads them to do well at work and have a meaningful life.

Actions to Develop Children's Sense of Curiosity at Home

Here are some activities for your students to do at home with their families. Select the ones you feel families would enjoy and which would develop students' sense of curiosity most. You can reference them in emails to families or your class newsletter.

	Wonder Walk	Bring a tablet or notebook and teach children how to take notes on wonderings and observations.
	Book Basket	Create a basket of books on topics children are wondering about.
	Neighborhood Walk	Go on a walk around the neighborhood as a family and stop and jot down what you observe.
	Curiosity Window	Use tape and draw a box in a window; put markers and pens and index cards near the window so children can look out the window and take notes on what they see.
	Curiosity Tour	Together, create a list of family wonderings. Research these wonderings together online or with family experts.
	20 Questions	Ask family members to stand in the center of a circle of people and select someone to be like an animal or famous athlete. They can then act out the choice while members of the group guess what or who they are by asking yes and no questions. If the group members figure out what or who the family member is in 20 questions or fewer, they win the round.

Routines to Develop Children's Sense of Curiosity

- Keep a wonderings chart of children's questions; go online with children and find the answers together.

- Ask children questions that spark meaningful conversation.

- Ignite students' curiosity by taking them to a museum, park, or another place that relates to a book they have read.

- Have children keep a journal of wonderings and create a story based on their questions.

- Encourage children to read informational books about new or unfamiliar topics.

- Make observations about your surroundings when out and about with children.

- On slips of paper, record new words children discover and keep them in a word jar. Every now and then, take them out and discuss their meanings.

CHAPTER 7

STRENGTH FIVE: CONFIDENCE

"I am not afraid of storms, for I am learning how to sail my ship."

—LOUISA MAY ALCOTT

When Tripp was about three and a half years old, he was sitting on his bed with his mom, and she said to him, "Read to me!" He looked up from one of his favorite books, *Dragons Love Tacos*, laughed, and said, "I don't know how to read! Read to me!" At the tender age of three, he already understood what it meant to decode the words on the page, to use his voice to represent various characters and moods, and to draw meaning from the illustrations. However, he also understood that he did not yet know how to attach the right sounds to the letters to read the exact words on the page. For a three-year-old, he shows an understanding of reading that may surprise us, and we may appreciate his continued confidence in his development as a reader.

A fourth-grade classroom in San Francisco is filled with desks for 32 students, bookshelves, computers, a pet hamster named Percy, book boxes, file cabinets, and a slew of art materials. The teacher is wondering where to move that one boy who continues to talk and disrupt his classmates. She knows he is having difficulty reading in the content areas, which have jumped in complexity and vocabulary, with fewer illustrations and photos to provide support. As soon as it's independent work time, the talking and distracting behavior starts. She moved him by Percy, but he continued to talk to Percy and disrupted the rest of the students. He is a sweet child, rather shy. She finally decides to sit him by her desk, but he is frustrated and angry and refuses to move. Before she can ask him one more time to move, he yells, "I CAN'T READ!"

The three-year-old and the fourth grader are aware of themselves as readers. They understand reading's ability to open or limit access to information or enjoyment, depending on the ability of the reader. The three-year-old is amused at being directed to read because he is not being judged on his ability to read. The fourth grader, who has been in school for four full years and two months, is acutely aware of himself as a reader. By the end of the school year, the fourth grader was reading and writing nearly at grade level, thanks to intervention at LitCamp. Both boys have the ability to learn and thrive and become successful readers. The three-year-old is confident in his ability to grow, but for a fourth grader, after years of watching peers develop as readers and move so far ahead of him, it is reasonable to see why he has lost confidence. Confidence leads to risk taking, which leads to growth. How can we ensure that students grow in their confidence as they continue to grow in their competence? We nurture both.

Why Confidence Matters

Often schools perceive unmotivated readers as kids who do not value reading, when the real problem is that the students lack confidence in themselves as readers. When students' confidence as readers increases, so does their motivation and, ultimately, their reading achievement. Studies by Gallup (2014) and the ACT (2014) reveal that students' educational aspirations are universally high, regardless of income or background. Guthrie (2013), as quoted in Harvey, et al. (2021), stated that "believing in yourself is more closely linked to achievement than any other motivation throughout school. Confidence, which is belief in your capacity, is tied intimately to success." Students want to succeed, and they generally know that becoming an accomplished reader—a super reader— is key to that goal.

Social psychologists who study motivation tell us that what often separates motivated readers from unmotivated ones is that the latter group lacks the confidence, or the expectation of success, in the reading enterprise (Eccles & Wigfield, 2002).

In her book *When Kids Can't Read*, Kylene Beers discusses that stamina and enjoyment play an important role in confidence-building. When teachers and families are able to improve these confidences, they are also able to increase students' reading achievement, and, perhaps more importantly, they help to develop students' identities as capable and engaged readers.

What You Can Do to Promote Confidence in Your Classroom

 Tap the power of literature to help students find their confidence.

Literature inspires confidence by showing students how they can move from not thinking they can do something to knowing they can do it, that the impossible can be possible. Sometimes it seems that every book ever written is in some way about this idea, that literature is helping us travel those sometimes lonely journeys of our minds, where we are asking: "Can I make it through?" And a character, or a real-life hero, answers us: "Yes! You can." In *Forged by Reading*: *The Power of a Literate Life*, Beers and Probst note that "it has been said that books change us, and certainly they might, but perhaps it would be better if we thought not that books change us, but that books give us the opportunity to change ourselves" (2020).

Here are some ways particular kinds of text help build confidence in super readers:

- Books about ordinary characters getting through tough spots, and those daily challenges of childhood, sometimes funny ones and sometimes very serious ones. Books like *Brown Girl Dreaming* by Jacqueline Woodson or *My Very Favorite Book in the Whole Wide World* by Malcolm Mitchell show students that mastering confidence comes from support, or innovation. For others, as *Standing on Her Shoulders* by Monica Clark-Robinson exemplifies, confidence can come from the empowerment of a unique identity, a historical role model, or a member of your own family.

- Stories about real-life heroes in which their childhoods are explored and we understand that confidence is something they were always working on. They had to make their way in sometimes challenging places to achieve their sense of self, well-being, and confidence. These books include *Building Zaha: The Story of Architect Zaha Hadid* by Victoria Tentler-Krylov, *Chester the Brave* by Audrey Penn, or *Planting Stories: The Life of Librarian and Storyteller Pura Belpré* by Anika Denise. They remind students of the power of their unique voice and the impact of using it, even when they feel like no one can hear.

- Graphic novels and/or comics in which characters triumph over seemingly insurmountable odds by nurturing their own confidence—books like *Niño Wrestles the World* by Yuyi Morales or *Rebel Girls Lead: 20 Tales of Extraordinary Women* by Elena Favilli and Francesca Cavallo. Readers tackle each challenge alongside these characters, leaning on and learning about confidences with each new twist.

- Informational articles that help students see moments of confidence, including interviews with athletes, conversations with scientists pursuing an idea, and sharings of writers talking about how they have to work their way through insecurity and their lack of confidence. The writer Ta-Nehisi Coates said, "When I was done with that book, it was clear to me it was not something I could have done before. Breakthroughs come from putting...pressure on yourself...and hoping you will grow some new muscles. It's not mystical....it is repeated practice over and over and you become something you had no idea you could really be."

 ## Focus on the role of speaking and listening in a super reader's life.

As Carmen Agra Deedy once said, "it's about having a voice...that's what we want for our children." Confidence is about practicing the power of your own voice in response to what you read and learning to trust in your voice. Students are practicing this from the start. Let us create classrooms where students have a great deal of opportunity to voice alternative viewpoints, to engage in genuine debates, to add new ideas to a conversation in an atmosphere of enjoyment and comfort. As Gholdy Muhammad (2020) notes, this often means having the space in the classroom that "nurtures criticality": "Students need spaces to name and critique injustice to help them ultimately develop the agency to build a better world." Confidence grows through active speaking and also active listening—the capacity to hear another's point of view and not be intimidated by it. Students can learn from leadership techniques to boost their own confidence, studying great leaders' speeches and interviews on YouTube and analyzing where the speaker/leader showed confidence and what strategies led him or her there.

So, too, the super reader is unafraid to ask an open-ended question herself. The best questions often do not have one answer but lead the conversation in interesting directions. Conversations about texts are a great way to practice confidence building, hearing one's own voice, and putting ideas into the world. You can model sentence starters that encourage all classmates to recognize their own confidence and to bolster it in others:

- I want to hear more of what you are thinking.
- Can we add on to your big idea?
- I like what you are saying about this text. Can you say more?
- I would like to respectfully challenge your idea with my own. Then let me hear more from you.

Recognize the power of collaboration in building confidence.

A community supports trying and recognizes the fact that sometimes failing builds a child's confidence. Partners and small groups make it possible for shy students to express their views. The use of Turn and Talk and Stop and Jot can also be extremely helpful in getting those quiet voices going. (See Chapter 12 for more information on these techniques.) And really valuing listening as an art form also contributes to a quiet child's confidence. Sometimes the most talented leaders are the best listeners. Schools don't always value that skill, although it is highly regarded by all the state standards. Listening to a read-aloud or listening to one another should be prized and affirmed. When we use statements like these, we send a message that we value students who are creating successful structures with their active listening stance:

- I love the way you leaned in during that Turn and Talk.
- You really noted the writer's craft in the read-aloud because you were listening deeply.
- You were a great partner today because you made it possible for your partner to go deep in her thinking.

In this era, performance-based work is valued and provides an opportunity to build readers' confidence. Giving students a chance to design and build something that may take many attempts to get right builds their confidence. The "failures" are natural and normal and will require new research, note-taking, and conversations each time in order to improve the work. Sometimes students may have the impression that there is only one right answer. But, in fact, a super reader learns that literature response may have many different interpretations and that collaboration helps them hear other perspectives and develop new ideas.

CONFIDENCE FOCUS LESSON

Your Own Superheroes

By having super readers create their own superheroes, you can encourage them to develop the confidence they need to be independent thinkers and express their ideas boldly.

Directions

1. Introduce the lesson by leading a conversation with your students about confidence. Ask students what confidence means to them. Feel free to use this definition to inform your discussion: *Thinking independently and expressing ideas with assurance.*

2. Explain to students that they will now create superhero versions of themselves. You can say:

   Thank you all for sharing your thoughts on confidence. I loved hearing your ideas! Now, I want you to keep that conversation in mind for our next activity: We're all going to create superhero versions of ourselves. You are all powerful in your own way, and you should have the confidence to show it when we read and learn together.

3. Tell students they will answer four questions about themselves as superheroes before creating their final Superhero Profiles. Read the questions aloud, and also be sure to write them somewhere in the room where students can read them. You can say:

   First, let's all quietly imagine superheroes in our heads. (Give them 30 seconds to use their imaginations.) *Now, picture yourself as a superhero! I'm going to give you four questions to think about:*

   - What does your superhero self look like?
   - What are your superpowers?
   - Who is your sidekick, or the person who helps you fight your battles?
   - What injustice do you fight? What problems do you hope to solve?

- Clarify each question by discussing them in-depth and providing an example for each. You can say:

  For the first question, think about yourself as a superhero. Include your costume and something that represents you as a superhero. You should show off your superpowers, or the reasons you are confident. I'm drawing myself with big ears because I'm a great listener. My hero has hearts all over the costume because I am super kind.

  For the second question, it's okay to include fantasy superpowers like flying or invisibility, but also be sure to include some superpowers that help you as a learner and reading community member—for example, "I can travel through time, and one of my learning superpowers is being great at remembering facts and details."

  For the third question, think about your sidekick. How do you two work together? How does your sidekick support you? My sidekick is my little brother. He has big muscles because he is strong and protective. He always has my back.

  For the last question, focus on injustices and problems that might occur in learning communities like ours.

4. Once students have had time to answer these questions, help them create their Superhero Profiles. Each student should divide a sheet of paper into four sections, then draw and write in them based on his or her responses to the four questions. As you explain the activity, walk them through an example you have prepared in advance. You can, of course, do this online, too, if you have a good tech tool to create beautiful drawings and creations. You can say:

   Thank you everyone for doing some great brainstorming for your superheroes. Now we're ready for the next step! I'm going to give each of you a sheet of paper that you can divide into four sections for the four questions.

   You can now draw and write in each section to show your superhero selves! The top left square is for question one, the top right square is for question two, the bottom left square is for question three, and the bottom right square is for question four.

   Now, everyone can start drawing and creating their Superhero Profiles.

Of course, any of these activities can be done online, too, but we do love the "old-fashioned" pen and paper for activities like these, so your students can hang them around the room or take them home to do the same.

5. Once the Superhero Profiles are completed, invite students to share them. You can have students share with the class, in small groups, or in pairs.

6. After students have had the chance to share, lead a discussion about the activity. Some guiding questions include:

   - How did it feel to create a superhero version of yourself?

   - Did anything surprise you about your Superhero Profile?

   - How did you decide on your superpowers?

   - Did you learn something about another student from his or her Superhero Profile?

   - How can you bring your confident Superhero Profile to life in our reading community?

7. Be sure to thank students for a wonderful job on their Superhero Profiles and for a great discussion! Tell them that they are all truly superheroes for being brave and sharing about themselves.

8. As a homework extension activity, ask students to interview family members and have them talk about people who are "superheroes" to them.

Actions to Promote Confidence in the Super Reader Classroom

Proud Moments	Have students record or write ways they are growing their confidence and keep a sketchbook for a week that describes their observations of their changes.
Power Booster	Have the students record how they will boost their confidence when they feel nervous or insecure. They do not have to share their Power Boosters, but they should use them in the future!
Constant Confidence	Build confidence as readers and speakers by allowing time for it every day. Allow for time in the day for students to read to the class.
Confidence Messages	Have all students write a note with praise for another student and distribute the notes. (Keep the notes anonymous, if possible.) Invite students to jot or record online a note of praise to boost confidence in others and share them. Make sure there is conversation about inclusion and caring (back to our strength of Kindness!) in recognizing all members of this community.
Confident Reflections	Celebrate confidence by having students read their favorite excerpts aloud from books and stories that share confident characters. Discuss these inspirations.

INTERACTIVE READING LESSON

Standing on Her Shoulders

by Monica Clark-Robinson
illustrated by Laura Freeman

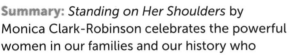

Summary: *Standing on Her Shoulders* by Monica Clark-Robinson celebrates the powerful women in our families and our history who have helped shape our contemporary world. This lyrical book reminds us that we are always a product of those who came before us.

Before Reading

Discuss Confidence:
- What is something you're good at?
- How might confidence help you in school? At home? With friends?
- Can you think of a time in your life when you felt very confident? Why did you feel that way?

Discuss the Book's Cover:
- What do you think this title and subtitle mean, and what might they have to do with confidence?
- What might some or all of the women in the picture frames on the first two pages have in common?

Vocabulary

Equality (n) the quality or state of being equal; the quality or state of having the same rights

Freedom (n) the power to do what you want to do; the ability to move or act freely

Peaceful (adj) untroubled by conflict, agitation, or commotion; quiet, tranquil

Champion (n) someone or something that has won a contest or competition, especially in sports

Grit (n) mental toughness and courage; or very small pieces of sand or stone

Think of the legends whose lives made way for yours.
Though years have passed, each story, each name endures.

When you speak their names, they live on in YOU.
You are standing on their shoulders, too.

Interpretation:
- What does the author mean when she says "...they live on in YOU. You are standing on their shoulders..."?
- How might seeing strong members of our family, and strong members in our history, help us to feel confident about our own abilities?

Author's Craft:
- What does the author and illustrator do to show the characters' inner thoughts?
- What might the young main character be feeling at this moment? Why?

After Reading
- What do you think is the relationship between empowerment and confidence? How might this story help you feel both?
- What are some historical figures, family members, teachers, or celebrities that help you feel confident?
- Who will stand on your shoulders?

▶ For other favorite books on confidence, see page 202.

What You Can Do to Promote Confidence at Home

You can support families in continuing this work at home. They have a tremendous opportunity to create a warm and supportive culture that encourages students to take learning risks and to see themselves as having a valued voice in the home and in the world. Confidence grows with perceived opportunities for success. The more kids feel that they are up for the challenge, the more confidence they will display.

Encourage families to give students ample time and space to practice confidence. Help family members to engage students often in conversation, asking them for their opinions of books they read and of current events. Give families confidence-building questions they can use that send the clear message to their children that their opinions matter.

- What do you think we should read tonight?
- How do you feel we should plan our homework schedule this week?
- I need your help. How might we solve this problem?
- When has your confidence grown this week? How did you observe that happening?
- How might you change the world? I am eager for your thoughts.

Actions to Develop Children's Sense of Confidence at Home

Here are some activities for your students to do at home with their families. Select the ones you feel families would enjoy and which would develop students' sense of confidence most. You can include these ideas in emails to families or in your class newsletter.

	Proud Moments	Have family members record or write ways they notice as a family they are growing in confidence together.
	Power Booster	Have all family members record how they typically boost their confidence when they feel nervous or insecure.
	Constant Confidence	Build children's confidence as readers and speakers by allowing time for reading and speaking every day. For example, set time every day for family members to talk about what they are reading.
	Confidence Notes	Have family members write anonymous notes of praise to one another.
	Confident Reflections	Invite family members to talk about what they are reading. They can describe the texts first, then offer their opinions on them.

Routines to Develop Children's Sense of Confidence

- Give children time to formulate opinions.
- Ask children to share favorite books or stories during family gatherings.
- Encourage children to practice using storytelling voices when sharing in family conversations.
- Invite them to read about a new passion and then share their learnings with multiple generations in the family.

CHAPTER 8

STRENGTH SIX: COURAGE

"I learned that courage was not the absence of fear, but the triumph over it."

—NELSON MANDELA

Ernest is sitting in the hallway outside of the Tom Bradley room on the 26th floor of Los Angeles City Hall with a group of kids who will soon be addressing the mayor, members of the California State Senate, educational leaders, the news media, and 200 other guests. These students are part of a summer program in which kids conduct research to address social issues in their neighborhoods and communities. Each summer culminates with a public presentation of the work. As Ernest scans the students who are in various stages of preparation and rehearsal, he sees a mixture of anticipation, excitement, and genuine fear. He calls the students together, and they begin to talk about why it is important to share their work. Some students comment that their research can change the way people think about kids. Others argue that they can change policies that affect their communities. Ernest responds that another important reason for them to share their work is that they will develop the courage to always speak their truth. Even in the face of fear, even in the face of overwhelming odds, those who have conviction and courage will know they can never be silenced. In Pam's community-based initiative, Books for Boys, she meets Daniel, who has been in many different foster care homes and has never found comfort in reading, until lately, when the Harry Potter books are read aloud. He says this is the first time he has met a character like him. When we ask him to share more, he says, "Harry Potter has a scar on his forehead, but I have a scar on my heart. Me and Harry, we have courage."

Why Courage Matters

Every day, children need courage, to grapple with the challenges of life, in themselves, in the home, at school, in life. Children's and young adult books are such beautiful ways to show our students that courage is possible, that even in the hardest of moments, your own internal strength can fortify you. There are many ways to define courage. These authors show us that it is in the small moments, too, that we see courage shine.

Children's and young adult books are such beautiful ways to show our students that courage is possible, that even in the hardest of moments, your own internal strength can fortify you.

Whether a child is learning a new difficult skill or reimagining her ability to tackle a challenge, risk taking and courage play important roles. Risk taking begins with a decision to act, and courage provides the inspiration to act. According to Michael Agar (1994), being courageous rewards individuals from living a life of "being" to a life of "becoming." Courage is critical for change and growth to occur.

In her research on children learning to write, Anne Haas Dyson (1995) celebrates the teachers and students in a third-grade class who find the courage to take risks and become superheroes of writing. Students wrote themselves into the narratives they created. They defied stereotypes, became the main characters, and were powerful. One student, Tina, became a superhero in her story as she developed into a superhero writer. As Dyson notes, "Tina's writing took courage, for it was writing that was clearly rewriting—shifting the constructed world and the possibilities of the constructed self in notable ways." When students courageously begin to view themselves as superheroes of

writing and reading, they transform from "being" to "becoming" and there are no limits to how far they can go and grow. As Malcolm Mitchell says, "All our children can read themselves into a better future."

Becoming a super reader requires courage in and of itself. Whether it is having the strength and perseverance required to tackle a difficult text or the will to act upon the things that we read that demand us to read actively, courage is key. When we speak of super reading as taking courage, we can share phonics and comprehension strategies that are the tools of the super reader kit, and we can make it clear that to face a tough page or screen requires fortitude. This helps a lot when a student is struggling. We are always looking through the asset lens and using language that affirms the struggle and the accomplishment. When we read about people who have had to overcome odds in life and work, the super reading we do makes us stronger. These days often do require courage, even to put one foot in front of the other. Our students of all ages will be inspired and renewed by your language that centers courage in their lives. They are heroes, too.

What You Can Do to Promote Courage in Your Classroom

Use super reading to activate a courageous spirit.

Books and stories—true and fictional, contemporary and historical—have extraordinary power to build worlds for students in which they can imagine themselves being courageous. They provide an example, yes, but also paint a picture of how a character or true-life person (or animal!) got to the point where he or she was able to do something outside her comfort zone. However the courage comes, from going on one's first overnight to standing up to a bully to rescuing people in a dire situation, literature tells our students the story of the human heart and spirit.

Give students the opportunity to categorize books by types of courage in the classroom library. Invite them to name the types of courage they have seen and experienced and the kinds they have read about. Some types may include:

- courage to stand up for what you believe in
- courage to fight for a cause
- courage to do something no one has ever done
- courage to take a risk
- courage to create a new idea
- courage to challenge the way things have always been done

Students can make baskets for these courage types or files if they are reading online. They can use the baskets/files to meet with "courage partners" to talk about what types of courage most resonate with them as they read.

Whether they're learning about a kind of quiet courage from Bernard Waber's *Courage*, ways to overcome obstacles from Kobi Yamada's *What Do You Do With an Idea?*, or ways to make a creative mark from Peter H. Reynolds's *Ish*, super readers can discuss how real and fictional heroes take steps to become who they are by having courage.

You can share great biographies about people who exhibit courage in their daily lives and also by doing things that are truly breathtaking, such as *So Tall Within: Sojourner Truth's Long Walk Toward Freedom* by Gary D. Schmidt, *On a Beam of Light: A Story of Albert Einstein* by Jennifer Berne, *When Marian Sang: The True Recital of Marian Anderson, The Voice of the Century* by Pam Muñoz Ryan, and *Frida Kahlo and Her Animalitos* by Monica Brown. The subjects of those books change the way we think about what "Yes I can!" means. They lead to rich discussion with students, especially if we keep the discussion open-ended by asking questions such as the following:

- Where does courage come from?
- What made it grow inside these characters?
- How is it growing inside you?

Connect courage to the learning that happens across subject areas.

This is a strength that shows up in many different ways as students are reading across the school day—from social studies to science to all the ways they are learning about the world and the people in it. Help students identify ways different fields—from math to art to music to history—have made leaps and bounds because people were not afraid to speak up, to challenge ideas, and to come up with new ones.

Create book sets of biographies of people who achieved a lot in their lives alongside copies of the actual work they did. Pair great picture books such as *Viva Frida* by Yuyi Morales alongside prints of Frida Kahlo's art. Pair *Martin's Big Words* by Doreen Rappaport with video of Martin Luther King, Jr. giving speeches or printouts of his original speeches for students to read.

Find heroes everywhere and study them.

In the book *The Courage to Care*, the rescuers in the time of the Holocaust share their stories, and the beneficiaries of their courage share as well. Max Rothschild, a German survivor of the Holocaust who was aided in his escape from the Gestapo by the Dutch underground, writes:

"In the fall of 1943, Niek Schouten, the one who saved my wife and me, dressed himself and a friend as Gestapo agents. They went on those bicycles with rubber wheels from house to house in a street in Rotterdam where Jews were living, and they said: 'We are from the Gestapo, and we have to pick up the children.' Then they put the children on the back of their bicycles and prepared to save them... In this way, they were able to save those children and many of us. Most of these rescuers consistently have refused to be honored. They cannot understand why they should be quoted, or cited, or given anything like a distinction of some kind or another. They want to forget about what they did during the war, and just go on... living the way they have always lived. That is their great beauty."

Think about how these quiet, unknown heroes rode the children on the backs of their bicycles. Think of how they refused to be honored. There is so much tender courage everywhere, always. Mr. Rogers said that in times of hardship, we should "look for the helpers." Children can study the quiet heroes, too.

Of all the strengths in this book, courage is perhaps the rarest to experience on a daily basis, and yet once experienced, or even read about, it can be intensely transformational. Reading gives the child the window to a world in which people act with moral justice, and also a world in which people don't. The absence of courage in our world has caused grave pain and sorrow. Even our youngest readers, whether reading a simple book such as *The Lion and the Mouse,* where a mouse heroically helps a lion, or hearing a story of a grandmother who took heroic measures for her family, can grow into the kind of people we hope will lead our world: our future civic, professional, and community leaders, of whom courage is expected and nurtured. As Martin Luther King, Jr., once said, "The arc of the moral universe is long, but it bends toward justice."

By building a super reader classroom, we are raising citizens, helpers, and courageous humans. Your work can indeed change the world, one super reader at a time.

Courageous Character Cards

By asking super readers to reflect on the actions and motives of brave characters in books, we encourage them to tap into the courage they need to overcome fears they have that may stand in the way of their learning.

Directions

1. Introduce the lesson by saying:

   Today we're going to do an activity to get us thinking about courage. Each of us will make a Courageous Character Card. But first, I'll give you time to think of a brave character from a book you've read and write about him or her.

2. Once each student has chosen a character, have him or her write a list of moments the character showed bravery. You can say:

   Now that you have chosen a courageous character, record some times this character demonstrated courage.

3. Help students create Courageous Character Cards. Then have them trade them with each other, taking the time to share in pairs how they are inspired by their characters. Distribute a sheet of unlined paper to students and have them hold it horizontally and fold it in half. Then, explain what will go on each side of the paper. You can say:

   On the left side of the paper, you can draw a picture of your courageous character. On the right side, you can write about all the times that character was brave. You can write this as a list, or you can jot down some short stories about the characters.

4. Invite students to share their cards with the whole class, and ask how they are inspired to take action in their own lives that is in the spirit of this character. Lead a discussion about the activity by asking questions such as:

    • Why did you choose this character?

    • Did the character feel afraid at all before acting with courage? How do you know?

    • If so, how do you think the character overcame his or her fear?

5. Connect the concept of courage to your reading community. Ask:

    • What are some things we can do to gain courage?

    • How can we help others in our reading community gain courage?

Actions for Promoting Courage in the Super Reader Classroom

Courage Badges	Create courage badges that have a symbol on them that the students select as an emblem that gives them courage.
Courage Time Line	Invite students to read about different historical figures and create a time line of courageous behaviors exhibited by these figures.
Courage Mirror	Have students write "mirror poems" to reflect their thoughts of people who inspire them in their own family or neighborhood.
Courage Commitments	Find examples of courage in the books you read and have students make courage commitments to changing the world or community based on what inspires them in the book they read.
News Hour	Share stories based on current events and ask the students to identify specific acts of courage. Discuss ways they can be courageous in their own lives.

INTERACTIVE READING LESSON

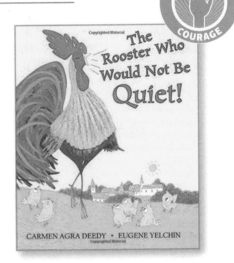

The Rooster Who Would Not Be Quiet!

by Carmen Agra Deedy
illustrated by Eugene Yelchin

Summary: When a new mayor prohibits a noisy town from making any noise, one proud rooster refuses to repress his song. In *The Rooster Who Would Not Be Quiet!* by Carmen Agra Deedy, a persistent rooster shows a town the courage it takes to stand up for what you believe in.

Before Reading

Discuss Courage:
- What does *courage* mean to you?
- Who have you read about that has shown courage?
- What is something you could do that shows courage?

Discuss the Book's Cover:
- What do you notice about this cover's illustration? Title? Word sizing? Colors?

Vocabulary

Village (n) a settlement usually smaller than a town

Shrugged (v) to raise or draw in the shoulders, especially to express uncertainty

Familiar (adj) frequently seen or experienced; easily recognized

Indigestion (n) inability to digest or difficulty in digesting something, marked especially by a burning sensation or discomfort in the upper abdomen

Interpretation:
- What do you notice about the rooster's personality? How does the author show the rooster's personality?
- Why is the rooster refusing to be quiet?

Dogs bayed,
mothers crooned,
engines hummed,
fountains warbled,
and everybody sang in the shower.

Author's Craft:
- What do you notice about the author's verb choice here? How does it paint a picture of the town? What do you see, hear, and smell in this town?
- How does the author use repetition in this story? How does that help the reader understand the characters?

"Still singing?" snapped Don Pepe. "You have no tree. Remember?"

"I have no tree," said the *gallito*. "But I have my hen and chicks. How can I keep from singing?"

"Will you sing if I throw you in a cage — alone?" threatened Don Pepe.

"I may sing a lonelier song," said the stubborn *gallito*. "But I will sing."

And he did.

After Reading
- How did the rooster show courage?
- What does it mean to believe in something, and what do you believe in?
- What is a rule that you value? How about a rule that feels unfair? Why?
- What would you stand up for?

▶ For other favorite books on courage, see pages 202–203.

Courage in Action

- Find video clips online that tell stories of courageous actions.
- Show students inspirational clips from courageous young people like Malala Yousafzai.
- Create short video reflections on what courage means to you.
- Find examples of daily courage at online news sources and share.
- Have your class record and edit a series of one-minute Public Service Announcements (PSAs) on the meaning of courage. Share the PSAs in a class-wide or school-wide assembly.

What You Can Do to Promote Courage at Home

Families have an important and unique role to play in building courage at home. You can support families by encouraging specific literacy-based activities that encourage the building of courage.

Help families select books that address themes of courage by sending home samples from the list on page 202. Encourage families to have conversations about the big ideas in the books. Send home conversation starters such as:

- What is your personal definition of courage?
- Where have you all seen examples of quiet courage in our community?
- Where have we experienced or witnessed courage in our family?

Invite families to develop a family definition of courage, and talk about how that definition might be the same or different from the way courage is portrayed in popular media. Have families make "Courage Goals" and hang them somewhere for the rest of the family to admire. Remind families to note and celebrate moments when members of the family demonstrated courage. Have families share "courage" stories from their own cultures and prior experiences. Post those stories on a class blog.

Actions to Develop Children's Sense of Courage at Home

Here are some activities for your students to do at home with their families. Select the ones you feel families would enjoy and which would develop students' sense of belonging most. You can include them in emails or your class newsletter.

	Courage Badges	Create a badge for children when they take a new positive step as a reader.
	Courage Time Line	Invite children to read about different historical figures and create a time line of courageous behaviors they see in those figures.
	Courageous Family	Look at old photos if possible and/or tell stories of elders and ancestors, celebrating their stories of overcoming together.
	Reflections of Courage	Have a family discussion about times each family member was courageous.
	Family Actions	Find examples of courage in the books you read or stories you tell. Make a plan to reach out in the community to help others in a way that feels inspired by your readings.

Routines to Develop Children's Sense of Courage

- Support children when they stand for a big idea and/or a friend.

- Point out examples of strong leadership in real life and in the books children read.

- Commend children when taking risks with reading new material. Let them know that it requires tremendous courage to become a super reader.

- Family members can share and discuss a story about a time in their lives when they took a risk and needed to show courage.

- Give children the opportunity to show courage by encouraging a new activity, such as a sport or dance.

- Celebrate moments of success and reflect on moments of failure as positive steps in growing. When discussing the meaning of success, focus more on courage and effort than on outcomes.

- Have children act out their writing or someone else's writing that speaks to a sense of courage.

CHAPTER 9

STRENGTH SEVEN: HOPE

"I believe in one day and someday and this perfect moment called Now."

—JACQUELINE WOODSON

A group of young adolescents are having a class discussion. Ms. Garcia, their teacher, has asked them to define a critical poem. One student offers that a critical poem is about changing the world. Ms. Garcia asks, "How does a critical poem change the world?" Another student comments that critical poems point to problems but that they also point to solutions to problems we face in society. Several students chime in making similar points about how critical poets go "deeper," and how they deal with serious issues in their poems. Sandra is a relatively new student in the class. She has been kicked out of her previous school, and her attendance to date has been sporadic. Up to this point, she hasn't added anything to the conversation, but she quickly shifts her body in a way that commands the attention of the class as she exclaims in desperation, "How can a poem change the world! I mean, can a poem really change the world?" The class is quiet and thoughtful, and a young woman sitting near Sandra responds, "What if that poem changes the poet, and then that poet changes the world? Then the poem changes the world, because it changes the poet." Sandra looks her classmate in the eye, and she is almost in tears. She whispers almost inaudibly, "Nice. I like that. The poet changes the world."

Moses is 10 years old. He came to New York City from Guyana the year before. The very first sentence he writes in his life is his memoir: "I was the lonely deaf." This memoir explained to the class how isolated his life was back home and how excited he is to be part of the community of new friends who understand him and who understand his loneliness. Moses loves science books, anything about the way the body works, and books about animals and nature. He browses and studies them carefully. Later in the year, he writes: "My name is Moses. I will become a doctor. I will take care of people." Moses, finding a home with others, reading his way to a deep understanding of his passions and his own strengths, writes from a place of strength: a world of hope.

When we instill hope in students, we help them to understand that they are powerful readers and thinkers and speakers and doers with so much to share with the world.

Why Hope Matters

Hope is a basic human need. When we lose hope, we lose our humanity. For more than two decades, Shawn Ginwright has worked with students who have experienced tremendous suffering in their lives. The difference, he argues, between the kids who are able to confront and ultimately overcome obstacles and those who are unsuccessful, is hope. To that end, he now makes teaching kids to hope the focus of his work with educators. His book *Hope and Healing in Urban Education: How Urban Activists and Teachers are Reclaiming Matters of the Heart* (2015) profiles successful educators and community leaders who are using reading and writing to instill hope in communities. Ginwright's message is powerful. Hope not only makes the difference, hope *is* the difference. When we instill hope in students, we help them to understand that they are powerful readers and thinkers and speakers and doers with so much to share with the world. Stories can bring hope in extraordinary ways. Recent research has shown that children who are told a story in a pediatric hospital "...showed lower levels of the stress-related hormone cortisol and higher

levels of oxytocin, which is often described as a feel-good hormone and is associated with empathy." They also "reported pain levels dropping" and "used more positive words to describe their hospital stay." (Cosier, 2021) Stories transmit hope. Children telling stories, sharing stories, and absorbing stories creates a culture of hope, one day at a time.

What You Can Do to Promote Hope in Your Classroom

Use super reading to promote hope.

The poet Emily Dickinson wrote that hope is "the thing with feathers," and that is really what stories do for students: they give them feathers to fly. The super reader soars over the difficulties of the day, thanks to the comfort that a wonderful story, an uplifting poem, or a funny comic brings. The super reader is visiting worlds where many hopeful things are possible. The "thing with feathers" is the story—the words on the page that send the super reader flying.

Of all the strengths, hope can be the most abstract, the most elusive, if we talk about it that way. Let stories show us the way. Consider organizing your classroom library around the ways we think about hope—or for what we typically hope:

- ourselves
- our families
- our community
- our world

All the texts we read with students can be framed around these lenses: self, family, community, and world. Invite students to look through those lenses when discussing a read-aloud, when working on their independent reading, and when working or talking in small groups or with partners.

Create a hope read-aloud collection. Let students know that when super readers get discouraged in life, they often turn to cherished texts that lift them up and inspire them. Poems such as "My People" by Langston Hughes, picture books such as *Owen & Mzee* and *The Adventures of Beekle: The Unimaginary Friend*, and chapter books such as *Bud, Not Buddy* and *The Crossover* can offer students a springboard to talk about times when hope prevails over sorrow or adversity.

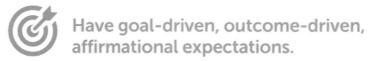

Have goal-driven, outcome-driven, affirmational expectations.

Hope is about celebration. There are times when we are working in places where life is extremely difficult for children—places where it seems there is no opportunity to experience the joy of hope at all. But students will always find a way. In our LitWorld projects, we see students playing with whatever they can find, making soccer balls from twine they collect, making castles from remnants of cardboard. They will always find a way to imagine a world of possibility, of the creative art of making things and building worlds. Children crave hope. They want hope. They need hope to thrive. In order for them to have hope, we have to practice it with them every day. And it is not only children experiencing deprivation who need this.

Hope is about feeling unique, necessary, and valued in the world, and how we translate that feeling to action and forward motion. Here are some ways to do that across the day with super readers:

- Set a personal, community, or world goal at the start of each week. Check in on that goal at the end of each week.

- Have a mini-celebration (with food if possible!) to share how the goal is progressing.

- Tap into how super reading is impacting those goals. If a personal goal is "I am going to be a better brother to my baby sister," what kinds of books can that reader collect and read in and out of school to foster that hope coming true?

- Keep a basket of Hope Stars. Add the stars to the walls of the classroom when you see a goal being accomplished that represents the larger hopes and dreams of your classroom community.

Help students dream big.

Every child, every teen, deserves a chance to dream, and to dream big. We can practice a hopeful mindset with students from the youngest ages. Dreaming big means making plans so hope feels purposeful, disciplined, and intentional.

If a child's dream is to become a doctor, have some of her reading and writing work be around that idea, and say to her, "I believe in this dream of yours. I want to help you think about it." Then, create reading baskets or online folders with ways for students to read about their dreams and to make lists, organize ideas, and interview people about their hopes. Maybe they want to start a lemonade stand. Maybe they want to invent something new. Maybe they do want to be a poet. Whatever that dream is, honor it, care for it, and make sure super reading is part of it. See how your students can connect the reading they are doing to the more hopeful mindset they are developing. If they read a book like *My People* by Langston Hughes, with photographs by Charles R. Smith; *Martin's Big Words* by Doreen Rappaport and illustrated by Bryan Collier; or *Eleanor, Quiet No More* by Doreen Rappaport and illustrated by Gary Kelley, they can work together in partnerships or small groups to build ideas and theories about how these amazing people began to create hope mindsets, and how those mindsets helped them to achieve great things.

You could also create dream catchers to hang in the classroom that show one big dream every child has. Give students a chance to change what's in the dream catcher at several times a year. Create Hope Folders online or offline where your students can keep a hope a day and revisit them at the end of the year. We can also ask the following:

- What will it take for you to go after your dreams?
- What kind of reading do you need to do here to make that happen?
- What might get in your way and how can I help you remove the obstacles to that?
- What would make you feel the most able to live your hopes and dreams?
- What quotes and sayings can we hang in the room or put into our online files to look at each day to make sure you feel inspired every day?

Remember, you may change the lives of your students with these momentous questions. Your children are never too young to begin living a hope-filled life, and they are never to old to start having one.

Hope Heart Maps

By having super readers create Hope Heart Maps, you can forge a strong connection between hope, reading, and goal-setting.

Directions

1. Introduce the lesson by saying:

    Even in the most difficult times, our hearts have corners of hope. Let's create maps today that reflect those golden parts of our hearts.

2. You can say:

    Along the top of your paper or screen, write the phrase "I am hopeful about." (Show an example.)

3. After students have made their lists, have them draw a heart.

4. Ask students to write the different hopes they have inside their hearts. Invite students to include hopes that they want to come true soon, as well as hopes for the future when they're grown up. Have them connect their hopes and dreams to what they have been reading about.

5. Invite students to decorate their Hope Heart Maps.

6. Be sure to leave a few minutes for sharing work and discussing the activity. Affirm their willingness to explore and share hopes. Guiding questions can include:

    *   Which hopes are most important to you?

    *   What is one way you can work on one of your hopes and/or dreams coming true?

    *   How can you help someone else's hopes and dreams come true?

    *   What can you read about next to further your hopes and dreams?

7. Display the Hope Heart Maps in your classroom or have students take them home to give to family members as gifts.

8. As an extension activity, invite family members to come together and discuss the words they put in their hearts and the positive changes they would like to see and make in the world.

9. Commit to a Hope Action in the community. Have students make a strategic plan for how to reach out to help others, and to sustain hope and enact it.

10. Invite students to write an op-ed, a speech, or a song that is about inspiring others to find hope in their lives. Have a Hope Celebration sharing the books that the students have read, and the writing they've done in response.

Actions for Promoting Hope in the Super Reader Classroom

Hope Goals	Set goals together as a class in an online document or on a poster. These goals can relate to reading as a hope-driven activity, including reading more, reading more independently, and making book clubs and partnerships that feel exhilarating and supportive.
Admire Hope	Invite students to choose a hopeful character from a book they have read, and write about how they can learn from him or her.
I Have Hope	Have students create specific personal reading goals, such as, "I want to read four new genres this year" and "I want to read for 15 minutes straight without getting distracted." Occasionally check in with students on their goals and help them set new ones.
Hope Wall	Invite students to think of something that they are hopeful about. Then, have them choose an image to represent it.
Stories of Hope	Have students listen to a speech, poem, or other presentation that you feel embodies hope. Lead a discussion about how the speech made them feel, and any lessons they can take from the speaker.
Hope Gifts	Have students find quotes, poems, and songs to share with others in the class (and home) that make them feel hope and that they would like to share with others to give them hope, too.

Martin Rising: Requiem for a King

by Andrea Davis Pinkney
illustrated by Brian Pinkney

Summary: In *Martin Rising: Requiem for a King* by Andrea Davis Pinkney, a collection of poignant and stirring poetry and captivating paintings beautifully tell the life story of Martin Luther King, Jr.

Before Reading

Discuss Hope:
- What does the word *hope* mean to you?
- When you think of *hope*, what other words come to mind?
- What are you hopeful for about the future?

Discuss the Book's Cover:
- What do the colors and paintings tell you about possible themes?
- Consider the title. Let's discuss it in the context of hope.

Vocabulary

Companion (n) one that keeps company with another

Boycott (v) to refuse to buy, use, or participate in something as a way of protesting

Privilege (n) a special opportunity to do something that makes you proud; or, a right or benefit that is given to some people and not to others

Sparkling (adj) to give off or reflect bright moving points of light

Eager (adj) very excited and interested

During Reading

Author's Craft:
- How does the author use the title of each poem to communicate the progression of the story?
- How does the author use white space and line breaks to communicate emotion?

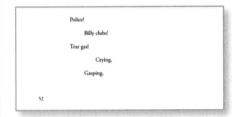

Interpretation:
- How does the illustrator use paint color to enhance the poet's words? And to communicate hope?
- What kinds of hope do you think the author is conveying by writing about Martin Luther King, Jr.'s life in this way?
- What small and big moments stand out for you and why do you think the author illuminated them?

After Reading
- In what way does the strength of hope inform the entire book?
- Let's discuss Martin's message. What kind of hope do you believe the author feels it gave the world? What do you think?
- What are your greatest hopes for yourself, your community, and your world?
- How could you bring them to life?

▶ For other favorite books on hope, see page 203.

What You Can Do to Promote Hope at Home

Encourage families to nurture the dreams and aspirations of their children. Remind families that reactions to their children's ideas and attitudes can mean the difference between a hopeful student and a disengaged student. Provide examples of ways families can support the positive spirit of a child at home.

- When students face challenges, families can encourage hope, resilience, and a belief that any challenge can be met by affirming the small steps the child took, and telling stories of one's own life to help the child envision a hopeful future.
- Make a notebook together or put a list on the refrigerator of a family "hope of the week."

Encourage families to nurture a sense of hope by bringing books into the home that focus on hope. For a complete list of books, see page 203. Suggest conversation starters to get discussions going at home that instill a hopeful point of view in students:

- Who makes you feel hopeful? Why?
- What hopes do you have for the future?
- What do you hope will happen today? Tomorrow? This year?
- How can you help someone else feel hopeful?

Encourage families to seek out models of hope and inspiration. Families can point to people in their family, in the community, and in their cultural history who stood for hope. Ask families to share biographies of great leaders who stood for hope and change.

Families can include hopeful sayings in the home as well, from people like Toni Morrison or Mahatma Gandhi, that speak to hope and being the change we'd like to see in the world.

Actions to Develop Children's Sense of Hope at Home

Here are some activities for your students to do at home with their families. Select the ones you feel families would enjoy and which would develop students' sense of hope most.

	Family Goals	Ask families to set goals: • Read a book together. • Do a family activity. • Have dinner together every night for a week. • Do something to help the community.
	Embody Hope	Invite family members to choose a hopeful character from a book, and write about how they can learn from him or her.
	I Have Hope	Develop a sense of hope after reading stories with characters who persevere through challenges. Talk about what hope means and why it's important to the lives of the characters.
	Hope Wall	Invite family members to think of something that they are hopeful about. Then, have them choose an image to represent it. Add the images to a poster that can be displayed in the home.
	Hope Stories	Share a poem, quote, or memorable saying from an elder or passed down from an ancestor and have a discussion about how these sayings still inspire the family to this day.

Routines to Develop Children's Sense of Hope

- Make a wish for the community, country, or world and share it with others.

- Find stories in the world about hope and optimism (on social media, in the newspaper, in what families read together). Ask children to make connections.

- Have conversations on goal setting for a variety of purposes: playing sports, learning at school, socializing with friends, engaging in civic activities, and so on.

- Talk to children about their hopes for the future. Have them set one concrete goal, and help them work toward the goal.

- Create a family story book (in photos, pictures, and/or words) that focuses on hope-driven ideas.

- Ask children to point out conflicts and resolutions in the books they are reading. What are the life lessons? How do the characters overcome their challenges?

- Have children express in writing their hopes for the community or for the world. Send their finished pieces to local community organizations.

- Ask your local librarian to create a list of books in which characters maintain hope in challenging situations.

Next Steps in the Journey

Now that you've had an opportunity to visit each strength up close, it's time to turn to Part II, which looks at the 7 Strengths Framework in action in the Super Reader Classroom. This section is full of best practices, strategies for how to implement independent reading, management techniques, and planning and assessment tools. By giving structure to the work that is often hard to pin down—the internal work our students do to become lifelong readers—we can impact our students for life.

PART II

THE 7 STRENGTHS FRAMEWORK IN ACTION

CHAPTER 10

BEST PRACTICES FOR SUPER READERS

We have built environments for super readers here in the United States and all around the world, and the amazing thing is that no matter where we go to establish these environments, students are seeking the same things: a sense of community, belonging, safety, trust, and engagement. There are concrete ways we can ensure that our classrooms can flourish. The classroom culture, discourse, and even physical setup all play key roles in fostering outcomes for super readers. In this chapter, we will discuss best practice teaching methods that strengthen all readers and how to implement them in your classroom.

Teaching Methods That Strengthen Super Readers

We can model what successful, engaged readers do, but also allow students extended time to apply and practice what they have learned about reading. Teaching structures, such as the read-aloud and small-group practice, teach students all the rules and tricks of super reading, and then the independent practice helps all students *play the game*.

No matter your setting, you can create what we call an accordion flow to your classroom management that creates opportunities for explicit instruction as well as independent practice. The following table describes the accordion teaching model we call "whole-small-whole."

Whole-Small-Whole Teaching Sequence (Can be done online, too!)	
Whole	Gather the entire class and use high-quality literature to model a skill or strategy and to build reading community values.
Small	Work with small groups, pairs, or individuals. The students apply and practice what they learned in the whole-group lesson. Coach students in their efforts and use this time to address the needs of individuals through conferences or small-group instruction.
Whole	Gather the entire class. Students share results of the independent and small-group work, reflect on how it went, and articulate why it was helpful to them as readers.

Read-Aloud

What Is It? A powerful and engaging reading of an authentic text chosen from a variety of genres and levels to an audience of one or more.

Why Is Reading Aloud Helpful to Super Readers? There are innumerable reasons why reading aloud is profoundly beneficial for super readers. The first is that it immerses our students in the sound of literary and informational text, giving them a chance to "marinate" in high-level vocabulary, grammar, and language structures. The second is that it gives you a chance to model what experienced readers do. Reading is so invisible to others on a daily basis; it is hard for our students to see exactly what we are doing when we are reading independently. But the read-aloud surfaces those skills and models for your students the ways we navigate pages, screens, and more. By reading aloud we can show students how we comprehend text, how we read fluently, and how we challenge ourselves with vocabulary. Finally, the read-aloud is a powerful invitation: an invitation to a lifetime community of readers, of the depth of feeling one gets by reading together, and all the ways we experience a world of stories and ideas as a community. We've identified two types of read-alouds in the super reader classroom, one in which we pause frequently to "teach into the text," which we call the instructional read-aloud, and the other, more informal approach designed to build that community and enjoyment of the reading experience, which we call the ritual read-aloud. We recommend at least one instructional read-aloud a day (at all ages) and two ritual read-alouds a day in a six-hour school day. These can range from a brief poem to an informational text to a chapter book.

Instructional Read-Aloud	Ritual Read-Aloud
• Offers opportunity for instruction in genre, strategy, fluency, and comprehension • Cultivates vocabulary development • Builds understanding and comprehension in texts • Exposes students to complex grammar	• Fosters a love of reading and models the processes of reading (stamina, enjoyment, engagement) • Immerses students in the richness of literary and informational texts • Introduces texts, genres, and authors to students

Reading aloud to your students stimulates the growth of the essential cognitive functions that lead to literacy development, such as narrative and informational text comprehension and visual imagery (Duke & Martin, 2015). Researchers have actually discovered that babies who were read Dr. Seuss before birth recognized the same text after they were born (DeCasper & Spence, 1986).

One study used functional magnetic resonance imaging to show how children's brains develop in relation to how much they had been read to at home. Children with more exposure to read-alouds had significantly greater activation in the areas of the brain responsible for visualization and multisensory integration (Hutton, Horowitz-Kraus, Mendelsohn, DeWitt, & Holland, 2015). Unfortunately, research also shows that many families stop reading to their children once they begin to do it on their own, yet the benefits of the family read-aloud can continue indefinitely (Trelease, 2006). Scholastic's 2016 report found the frequency of read-alouds "drops significantly after age 5 and again after age 8."

Reading aloud is a profoundly essential activity for reading success, particularly for emergent readers (Fisher, Flood, Lapp, & Frey, 2004). In 1985, the government report *Becoming a Nation of Readers* (Anderson, Hiebert, Scott, & Wilkinson) stated that "the single most important activity for building the knowledge required for eventual success in reading is reading aloud to children" (p. 23) and current research continues to support this finding (Lesesne, 2006). Children of all ages should be given the opportunity to participate daily in this high-joy, high-impact activity, at home and in classroom settings.

The read-aloud is how we make the work of reading "visible." Reading aloud is a skill and art, especially when we are sharing with children (Braxton, 2007). While there are specific suggestions for making a read-aloud as engaging and enjoyable as possible, such as introducing a story and building background knowledge, the most important way to excite children about reading and a particular text is to let inhibitions go, reread as needed, and be as expressive as possible. Read-alouds take on a few functions in the home: a 2016 Scholastic study found that "...two-thirds of parents (66%) say the read-aloud experience includes more than just the reader and the child, most commonly the child's other parent and/or siblings… punctuating that reading aloud is a tool for family bonding, inspiration, and education." Ultimately, as librarian and author Barbara Braxton suggests, "Reading aloud is such a simple pleasure, but it can be a complex task. If you enjoy yourself, however, the children will, too."

Families whose primary home language differs from the school language should be encouraged to read aloud in the language with which they are most comfortable. Skills, strategies, and a passion for reading can be taught in any language and research has consistently shown that "development of children's home language supports their learning of English" (Wiley & de Klerk, 2010, p. 403; Espinosa & Ascenzi-Moreno, 2021; Lopez-Robertson, 2021, Vu, 2021). According to Espinoza & Ascenzi-Moreno (2021), "far too often, emergent bilinguals are asked to wait until their English is good enough to fully engage in the transformative vision for reading and writing that we aim to provide for all students. Or, they are asked to leave key aspects of their language repertoire at the classroom door. Emergent bilinguals' language differences, cultural resources, and educational histories are often seen as challenges rather than as assets in their learning." Families can be supported in locating printed and digital multimedia texts in their home language and encouraged to help their children grow as super readers in multiple languages.

The stunning fact of the research is this: children who are read aloud to on a daily basis consistently outperform their peers, reaching levels almost a year ahead of children who are not read aloud to (Kalb & van Ours, 2013). In the classroom, when students actively listen to a read-aloud rather than participate round-robin style, they benefit from the teacher's modeling of fluency and the immediate engagement of hearing a wonderful story told well. Not only are children expanding their oral vocabularies, they are learning new concepts in a pleasurable way (Blachowicz & Fisher, 2015). Recent research suggests one advantage of read-alouds is the ways it familiarizes students with "decontextualized language, requiring them to make sense of ideas that are about something beyond the here and now" (Beck & Sandora, 2016; Beck & McKeown, 2001; Scharer, 2018; Laminack, 2019). The read-aloud invites children to sink into the world of a book and to flex the muscles of their imaginations as the story plays out in their minds.

The 7 Strengths and the Read-Aloud

- Bring the 7 Strengths to the forefront by reading aloud books that connect to each strength.

- Recognize when the 7 Strengths emerge as central ideas in your read-alouds.

- Acknowledge how reading aloud together brings us closer as a community and fosters a sense of belonging.

- Encourage students to express curiosity about the content of texts by asking questions about the content and illustrations and making and confirming predictions.

- Satisfy students' curiosity by prompting them to research and read aloud the answers to the class to their many questions about the world as they come up.

- Help students build courage to read aloud with fluency and expression in front of others.

- Have students turn and talk about their hopes and dreams before, during, and after the read-aloud.

- On the first Wednesday of every February, celebrate World Read Aloud Day with Scholastic and LitWorld (litworld.org), raising up your students' voices by inviting them to select their favorite 7 Strengths books to read at home with their families, and having an in-school celebration to proclaim the official magic of the read-aloud for all ages.

Text Investigations

What Is It? Reading at increasing levels of comprehension, from basic understanding of the text's message to understanding its structure, craft, and style to understanding its purpose and theme.

Why Are Text Investigations Helpful to Super Readers? Super readers are critical readers. They read carefully and thoughtfully, asking critical questions of the texts they read. It is powerful to create the contexts in which students become close and critical readers. For example, Ernest sometimes has his students participate in mock trials and debates based on the literature they read. Because they know that they will be responsible for all of the material covered in the book, they generally read it more carefully. Also, when students are reading as part of research for a report that they are going to share with an audience, they tend to pay close attention to detail.

Text investigations give you the chance to linger over text with your students to allow for deeper and more analytical understandings of key pieces of literature and informational text. You get the chance to model *what*, *how*, and *why* we read. Immersing your students in interactive reading experiences gives them the opportunity to learn the "look" and "feel" of language, to practice code breaking and meaning making together, to see the process of reading made visible. Students become strong, bold readers, approaching even the most difficult texts with new confidence in their abilities to decode what an author is trying to convey.

Text investigations can happen during whole-class instruction, small-group lessons, and conferences with individual students. Deep analysis should be done with complex texts, therefore interactive reading experiences need to be very scaffolded (and work best in small-group or one-on-one conferences).

Text Investigations Protocol for All Grades and Genres	
Preview	Examine the overall form and features of the text.
Read for what the text says	Try to summarize what the text is mainly about. Clarify unknown words.
Read for how the text is written	Analyze the author's choices of structure, words, and phrases to deepen your understanding of the text.
Read for why the text is written	Determine purpose and central ideas of the text.

Examining author's craft is a crucial part of text investigations. Our students studied why Ezra Jack Keats decided to make the boy's coat red in *The Snowy Day* and why he never named his character. One child said: "I believe Mr. Keats used only pronouns because he wanted us to feel like we could be the boy." Another child said: "I am a close reader of the footprints in the snow. Are they going forward or away? Maybe Mr. Keats wanted us to wonder." A third said: "I love how he used white space. It was like the snow itself, so quiet on that winter's day."

Encourage students to use text evidence to support any claims or conclusions they have about a text. See chart below.

Explaining Thinking Using Text Evidence	
Phrases to scaffold readers when they share their thinking orally and in writing: • I think this because ____. • The author shows this on page ____ where it says ____. • There is proof of my thinking on page ____. • There is evidence of this on page ____ where it states that ____. • In the ____ (e.g., text, photo, article, letter, chart, cartoon, graph, speech, etc.), the author/artist states/shows ____. • This idea is supported by the ____ (e.g., text, photo, article, letter, chart, cartoon, graph, speech, etc.). [Explain how.] • An example from the ____ (e.g., text, photo, article, letter, chart, cartoon, graph, speech) is ____.	**Other phrases to cite evidence:** • This clearly proves that ____. • It is obvious that ____. • Clearly, ____. • It is evident that ____. • This demonstrates ____. • This makes it clear that ____. **Other useful verbs for explaining why a source supports your ideas include:** *shows, conveys, justifies, supports, exemplifies, suggests, illustrates, displays.*

The 7 Strengths and Text Investigations

- Encourage students to be curious about the choices authors make. Word choice, character development, plot development, illustration details, and more are thoughtfully included to impact the meaning of a text. When reading closely, super readers consider why authors shape these literary elements the way they do.
- Have students do text investigations in partnerships or small groups where reading friends can help each other by collaborating on ideas.
- Help students build the confidence to do the hard work of comprehending challenging text.
- Model and practice kindness toward all readers in the class regardless of skill level. Students will engage in interactive reading experiences and all reading activities with varying levels of success. We are all growing as readers alongside each other.

Phonics and Word Explorations

What Is It? A time when students can practice their word building, decoding, and fluency skills on their own or in small groups or whole class for inspiration and motivation.

Why Is Phonics/Word Exploration Helpful to Super Readers? As longtime literacy educators, we are equally excited by and interested in the ways children architect language and phonetically and phonemically work with text. Every day should have opportunities for practice on these aspects of super reader growth. In this period of the

Phonics and Word Builders 7 Strengths

Belonging	Recognizing word families, grammar rules, morphological connections
Friendship	Working together in partners to decode and encode together
Kindness	Show kindness to oneself and others as you tackle hard words
Curiosity	Traveling through the world of reading with an open mindset
Confidence	Tackling hard words and word sets with fierce determination
Courage	Seeking out higher level vocabulary and new learnings about morphology and phonemic discoveries
Hope	Having aspirations and plans for what the future holds in terms of writing (encoding) and reading (decoding) at higher and higher levels

day, students can practice phonemic awareness and letter instruction, and development of knowledge of phonemes in spoken words and the link to letter recognition. As we have said before in this book, reading is like breathing in and writing is like breathing out, so the connections in this work between decoding and encoding are crucial and exhilarating. By writing, our students become more aware of the purpose of spelling, word part analysis, and more.

Time for Writing

What Is It? Daily practice as super writers, making those "reading is breathing in, writing is breathing out" connections, and making writing a lifelong habit readers have.

Why Is Writing Helpful to Super Readers? Every day, our students who are super readers are thinking about and considering the amazing connections between reading and writing: first, to absorb the world of reading as vocabulary curators, grammar champions, and story structure mavens; second, to practice the mechanics of language, from spelling (encoding) to using phonological awareness and knowledge of morphology and more to help them craft and exhilarate in the ideas they have and want to share; third, to learn about genres and styles of writing from the best of the best, the children's and young adult authors we have shared here in this book. Our students who are super readers are excited to create. They are like bakers, tasting the morsels of delight and then craving the opportunity to make their own. Decoding becomes encoding, comprehending becomes creation, sharing ideas becomes sharing writing products. Reserve at least twenty minutes a day for writing time. Use the 7 Strengths to guide you as a teacher of writing in exactly the same way we are doing for our super readers. Our students will flourish in a strengths-based writing community, too.

Small-Group Instruction

What Is It? A meeting with two or more students in which the teacher helps them achieve shared learning goals as readers.

Why Is Small-Group Instruction Helpful to Super Readers? The most effective small-group instruction occurs when you start with formal or informal data to match students with similar needs together. You then convene a manageable group of two to seven students to engage them in a lesson focused on a skill or strategy that they need. Meeting with small groups allows you to differentiate instruction effectively and efficiently. Students get more direct attention than during whole-class instruction, and you have the opportunity to choose texts and teaching objectives that closely address the needs of the group members. In small groups, students benefit from hearing the questions and ideas of fellow group members and solving challenges with and for each other.

This is also a time when students can work together, in pairs, or on their own with the support of the group on phonics, phonemic awareness, and phonological aspects of language. This work requires highly specific matching of students' strengths and needs, and therefore is best done in small groups and pairs and one-on-one so each student gets exactly what he or she needs in the order he or she needs it. Use the 7 Strengths language to describe the different elements of this work as well. For example, we can discuss how words belong to word families and word clusters, and we can discuss how to be curious about word etymologies, sounds, and patterns. We can engage students in practice around confidence- and courage-building to break through the hard parts of decoding and encoding. We can show friendship and kindness to those who may not be progressing as rapidly as we are; and kindness to ourselves when we stumble. Finally, we can discuss with our students how to create hope goals for this work of practicing the structures of language.

The 7 Strengths and Small-Group Instruction

- Students should treat each other's mistakes with kindness and be able to make mistakes while practicing confidence building.
- Urge students to work through challenges in small-group reading. Students should treat each other's mistakes with kindness and be able to make mistakes without losing their confidence.
- Help students recognize that working in small groups often allows them to build the courage they need to be successful as independent readers. Recognize their growth and teach toward independence.

Collaborating With Peers: Reading Partners

What Is It? A meeting of two students reading and discussing their reading together.

Why Are Reading Partners Helpful to Super Readers? The super reader loves to talk about her reading experiences. And she is listening, too. The partnership structure, even two times a week, is a valuable way for students to practice speaking and listening to each other about books. These partnerships can be flexible, changing each week or each month. They can be partnerships based on the following:

- interests
- favorite authors
- similar reading level
- similar reading challenge
- similar reading goal
- primary language
- project-based learning

Reading partners may happen in a variety of contexts: as quick meet-ups at any point in the day to check in on each other's reading or share something read outside of the classroom, during whole-class instruction as a Turn and Talk, or during small-group instruction or independent reading. This is a highly flexible structure that should come to feel natural for students so they can feel supported by a partner whether or not they are reading the same book. Scaffold students' conversations by providing and role-playing with conversation stems such as those in the chart that follows.

Crafting Longer and Stronger Conversations		
Describe	• I noticed that... • I see that...	• I hear you saying...
React	• I agree/disagree because... • This makes me feel _____ because... • I think _____ because...	• That's amazing/cool/funny... • This reminds me of...
Question	• I am wondering... • Why is...? Why does...?	• Why did the (author, poet, creator, photographer, illustrator)...?
Evaluate	• I like how... • I do not like how... • My favorite thing is...	• I really enjoyed... • The most important thing is...
Clarify	• What did you mean? • Can you explain?	• I feel confused about... • I don't understand...
Draw Conclusions	• This gives me a clue that... • I think that the message is...	• This teaches a lesson about...
Speculate	• I think that maybe...	• I am guessing that...
Expand	• What do you think? • Tell me more about that. • Let me add to what ___ just said...	• That's true... plus... • I also (noticed, thought, wondered)...

You can strengthen partnerships using the 7 Strengths language, such as:

	Belonging	I greet my partner with a welcome.
	Friendship	I share a connection with my partner when discussing books.
	Kindness	I am helpful and humble when working with my partner on the tough parts of reading.
	Curiosity	I ask questions about my partner's ideas that feel supportive.
	Confidence	I affirm my partner's small and big steps forward as a reader.
	Courage	I am brave in expressing ideas with my partner, and I am brave in hearing ideas that won't always match mine.
	Hope	I set positive reading goals with my partner.

Collaborating With Peers: Reading Clubs

What Is It? Small groups of students reading a shared text and engaging in discussion about it.

Why Are Reading Clubs Helpful to Super Readers? This is a wonderful way for your students to have longer sustained conversations and to get to know each other as readers. The club should, like partnerships, have a start and end date, and the same students should not be expected to stay together in one club all year. It is to mix the levels of students so they can experience different kinds of conversation. For example, a club could meet for a week to talk about poetry, or the club could meet for two weeks to talk about the theme of bullying. In these two cases, the club does not have to commit to reading the same text at the same time.

These clubs can be done virtually, too. Organizing them around the 7 Strengths makes it really fun to see progression and to structure conversations. Also, you are sending the message that this is an asset-based environment and that conversations about reading welcome and include all voices. In her book *Classroom Discourse: The Language of Teaching and Learning*, Courtney Cazden (1988) identified that most classroom talk was initiated by and directed toward the teacher.

The 7 Strengths and Collaborating With Peers

- Develop a sense of belonging by helping students find peers to talk with about reading.

- Help students develop friendships that relate to the characters they read about—showing them a way to work through conflict and challenge with the great examples we find in reading. Encourage them to share wonderings with each other, building a culture of curiosity.

- Build students' confidence and courage by calling attention to the small steps they take in grappling with hard words, finishing a longer text, talking when shy, and more.

- Spread hope by letting students know they are trusted members of the community and that their engagement with a particular text, type of text, or idea is truly valued and important.

Creating an Environment That Supports and Engages Super Readers

Increasing reading engagement is essential to increasing literacy achievement and developing lifelong readers. We can define engagement as delighted, motivated, joyful, and resilient. In the super reader classroom, we see that engaged readers do far better on everything involving reading, including standardized tests and more. They see these things as worthy challenges, even if they'd rather curl up on the weekend with a graphic novel than a test! The idea of engagement is not "soft"—it's a huge part of what helps a super reader succeed. The 7 Strengths are a framework for engagement. Each of the strengths helps students to name what might be getting in their way and helps them to activate their inner resilience for the times when engagement is not easy. In the super reader classroom, if students are practicing phonics or phonemic skills, comprehension, or vocabulary, they can use the lens of the 7 Strengths to create discipline around their struggle and their delight—it's a framework that guides them in the light and in the dark.

In his 2004 *Journal of Literacy Research* article, John Guthrie describes a study of third graders and their literacy engagement. He found that 9-year-olds whose family background was characterized by low income and low education, but who were highly engaged readers, substantially outscored students who came from backgrounds with higher education and income, but who themselves were less engaged readers. Guthrie also found that engaged readers spend up to 500 percent more time reading than disengaged readers. He encourages families and teachers to increase reading time by 200–500 percent and to foster engagement through conceptual themes, hands-on experiences, self-directed learning, interesting texts, classroom discourse, and time for extended reading. Engagement continues to prove essential for student success. A 2021 study that spanned 11 countries found curiosity and persistence "were the strongest predictors of academic success in both math and reading for both children and teenagers" (Sparks, 2021).

The following practices are designed to foster a classroom culture that celebrates reading and helps to create a classroom environment that nurtures the growth of super readers.

How We Use the 7 Strengths

Belonging	We work together to create a learning community that explores the world and all kinds of literature.
Friendship	We bond because of our shared passions. We become super readers by working together and learning from one another.
Kindness	We support one another, working together to reach new heights as readers. We support one another with tenderness, care, and empathy, moving each other along the super reader pathway.
Curiosity	We feed our curious minds by asking and answering questions about what we read.
Confidence	We practice reading every day, using new strategies and skills to help us become fearless and strong.
Courage	We understand that reading can be challenging and aren't afraid to work through the hard parts.
Hope	We set goals for ourselves as readers and use those goals to think about the future.

Awareness Building

What Is It? Instruction aimed at building students' awareness of their preferences, habits, strengths, and challenges as readers.

Why Is Awareness Building Helpful to Super Readers? First and foremost, we strive to help all of our students recognize themselves as readers, regardless of age, skill level, language proficiency, or any other classifications that cause students to consider themselves outsiders from the group that calls themselves "readers." We are all on different places in our unique reading journeys. We can help our super readers right from the beginning continuously formulate their awareness of their changing selves and growth as readers. For the older readers who have not considered themselves to be super readers, this awareness allows them to "rewrite" that story every day, changing the narrative from deficit to asset, from failure to success.

Questions to Help Build Awareness in Our Super Readers

- What do you like to read about?
- Who is a favorite author right now?
- Where do you like to read?
- What is easy for you as a reader?
- What is challenging for you as a reader?
- What goals do you need to work on to become stronger as a reader?
- What kinds of books do you like to read?
- What genres would you like to explore next?
- What mode of reading is best for you, on- or offline?

The 7 Strengths and Identity Building

- Assure students that all students in the classroom are readers and belong to the classroom reading community.
- Help students develop curiosity about authors, genres, and books through engaging library displays, book talks, and peer recommendations.

- Provide frequent opportunities for students to share their reading preferences and make recommendations with confidence to their reading friends in the group.
- Satisfy students' hopes to grow as readers by helping them set goals and monitoring progress toward them.

Reading Celebrations

What Is It? Recognition of achievements, both small and large, of each student in the classroom, and the work that he or she does.

Why Are Reading Celebrations Helpful to Super Readers? Every day, be sure to find something you admire in students as readers. The goal is that by the end of the week, each student will have heard at least one specific thing about his or her growth as a reader. Be as specific as you can, for example: "Bobby, I so appreciated how you worked with your partner."; "Sarah, I really liked how you got comfortable quickly in your reading spot this week."

Celebrate students as readers by honoring each small step, for example: "I admire how you read in a one-inch voice so that others could read quietly." "I liked how you reread that passage when you didn't understand." "I observed how hard you worked to decode that hard word." These are teachable moments.

Have weekly reading celebrations. Use the opportunity to have students read to a guest or have a guest reader join the class for the day. Let the weekly celebrations celebrate small steps: that a read-aloud had longer discussion, or a child felt that she read for more minutes. Have students share out their gains in these ways. Some of the ways you can celebrate include:

Stamina: We read for more minutes this week.

Volume: We read many words this week.

Engagement: We were focused on our reading this week.

Comprehension: We had great book talks this week.

Growth: We changed and grew as readers this week.

Collaboration: We worked well with our partners this week.

The 7 Strengths and Reading Celebrations

- Recognize students' accomplishments, even their smallest accomplishments, to develop a sense of belonging.
- Cultivate a culture of affirmation; build a spirit of kindness for all.
- Deepen friendship by encouraging students to interact and engage with peers as readers (not only as playmates).

- Inspire hope by creating an atmosphere of enjoyment and pleasure around the reading experience.

The Classroom Library (online and books in hand)

What Is It? Exemplary texts that are used as models.

Why Are Classroom Libraries Helpful to Super Readers? A classroom library provides super readers with the most critical tool we can give them—texts to read. Readers thrive by reading. A curated collection—one with a variety of levels, genres, titles, topics, languages, and media—enables students to find texts that suit their interests and needs.

Students should have plenty of texts to choose from all year long. Bins clustered by genre, author, and topic help students find books they need and want to read. If students use tablets, be sure you create time to organize how students integrate both online and offline reading into library routines. Engage students in helping to organize the library. One easy way to do this is to allow them to form "Our Favorites" baskets with their favorite trade books or baskets of their own writing or folders or tags online, all to encourage others to read.

Text Types to Consider for Your Classroom Library			
Narrative	**Informational**	**Opinion/Argument**	**Poetry**
• Fairy tales • Myths • Graphic novels • Science fiction • Fantasy stories • Poetry • Realistic fiction • Historical fiction • Short stories • Memoir • Blogs	• Primary source documents • Reports • Informative picture books • Blogs • Biographies • Journal articles • Infographics • Functional texts • Scientific texts • Mathematical texts • Magazine articles • Websites • Historical texts • Maps	• Editorials • Reviews: product, music, film, book • Blogs • Social media posts • Letters to the editor • Advertisements	• Odes • Sonnets • Free verse • Haiku • Cinquains • Couplets • Songs • Lullabies

The 7 Strengths and the Classroom Library

- Value friendship by creating opportunities for sharing books and reading together.
- Honor kindness by flagging books that show us how to be kind and caring.
- Build confidence by grouping books of different levels together about similar interests so students can practice reading harder books on subjects they love.
- Create an online folder or have sticky notes available for students to create courageous comments about ideas they have about books.
- Have students respond to books in the library by answering the hopeful question: How could reading this book change your life? Change the world?
- Highlight belonging by including texts that capture the mirrors and windows of human experience.
- Deepen curiosity by offering students a diverse and interesting collection.
- Develop curiosity by including texts that are not commonly found in classroom libraries, but students love to read because they truly reflect their interests, such as sports books and silly joke books.

Mentor Texts

What Is It? Well-written texts that are used as models to influence students' reading and writing, or to inspire students personally.

Why Are Mentor Texts Helpful to Super Readers? To mentor is to teach. Super readers often have favorite texts that influence or inspire them in important and sometimes profound ways. For example, they may relate to a character or theme so strongly that they will articulate that the book changed their lives or the way they think about themselves. Informational texts may be mentor texts as well, especially those to which readers turn time and time again for knowledge that enhances some aspect of their lives. Some readers find a text they love so much that it provokes a turning point in their lives as a reader. They may even credit it for teaching them to read or making them think of themselves as readers for the first time.

Mentor texts may also impact a reader's writing life. All writers are readers. By definition, great writers have to be readers of others' texts and close and careful readers of the texts they create. Unfortunately, not all readers see themselves as writers and we'd like to change that. Ernest's life was forever changed by a fourth-grade teacher who allowed him to write his own novel. Pam's life was changed in the same way by her third-grade teacher who also allowed her to write her very own novel, *Thunder*, about a horse that looked and sounded suspiciously like Black Beauty! But she loved that book! As we allow our students to write in the artistic genres that they read, we will create the conditions for very close reading. When we've given the opportunity for fourth graders to write plays responding to social issues they'd like to change, they become very deep readers of plays as a way to learn the genre. They also become close readers of the news and of research that deals with social issues that matter to them.

Writers learn to write by noticing what authors do. Reading exemplar texts teaches them how to…

- Begin a story
- Teach something new
- Gather facts that build an idea
- Understand someone's feelings
- Make language beautiful

- Prove a point
- Build imaginary worlds
- Make a reader laugh
- End a story

The 7 Strengths and Mentor Texts

- Form book clubs based on favorite authors or genres (e.g., fantasy, historical fiction, comic books) to foster a sense of belonging.

- Encourage students to be curious about authors—why they write, where they get their inspiration, why they make the literary choices they do, and so on.

- Help students to develop the courage to try out new genres, styles, or topics inspired by their mentor texts.

Best practices become even better when they are rooted in the 7 Strengths. Teaching structures such as the read-aloud and reading celebrations will help you to build the 7 Strengths in your students.

Now let us turn to the super practice of all practices, the key ingredient to raising a lifelong super reader: the practice of independent reading itself. We gave this practice a chapter all of its own because we believe so much in the power of independent reading to change kids' lives. At LitCamp, the "bunk time" becomes every camper's favorite part of the day. It is a time of meaningful practice. Everything you have taught and everything you have done to raise a super reader crystallizes in this practice: they are on the field playing the game. It is often considered optional or supplemental, but as any super reader will tell you, this practice needs to be central; it is what turned them into lifelong readers. Let's find out how to integrate it into our instruction in magical, yet highly practical ways.

CHAPTER 11

STRUCTURED INDEPENDENT READING: THE SUPER PRACTICE

Independent reading is the time a reader spends actively engaged in reading a wide range of text, with active support and related instruction from the teacher. Recommended daily independent reading time—20 minutes a day in school, 20 minutes in the after-school program, and 20 minutes at home—adds up to one hour of transformational opportunity. Not bad for 60 minutes!

In the 7 Strengths Framework, independent reading is at the core of everything and is directly connected to instruction. Every minute students read allows them to develop a strong reading identity as well as stamina and fluency that leads to a lifelong love of reading.

Here, we have given a fresh name to this practice to give it even more power and centrality in the work we do. We have named this practice "Structured Independent Reading" to distinguish it from an informal, casual approach to the kinds of reading students might do on their own. This is really a way to consider the profound role SIR can play in the classroom, the "on the field" work the student reader does to build skills, strengthen reading muscles, and practice strategies and techniques that will make him a super reader.

The Importance of Choice and Access

The strengths-based classroom is all about centering the capacities of students. For this reason, choice is really important. Students need to be able to have time each day to explore their own passions, ideas, and interests as readers. If not, how will they know the purpose of reading? How will they really experience the joy of getting lost inside a book? The work of independence is about stumbling and trying again, and also about the sheer exhilaration of making a perfect match.

Students must also have access to a variety of diverse texts to read, ranging from easy, to just right, to difficult to decode, all of which have some purpose for the growing reader. Easy books provide a sense of ease and assurance, and give the reader's mind a chance to practice fluency. Books that match a student's independent reading level help the student practice comprehension, analysis, and enjoyment of texts. Difficult books that are of high interest help readers problem solve and practice dealing with challenges.

Of course, we all read for many other purposes than to practice reading, so students need these opportunities as well. It may be they are seeking information. It may be they need a book with a strong character to participate in a discussion about point of view. It may be they want to read a book their friend is reading. It may be they love an author and want to read everything the author has written. These aspirations are super reader dreams; build your classroom around super reader dreaming.

Providing students with opportunities for choice and access to abundant texts requires a purposefully organized classroom library. Scholastic's 2016 Family and Kids Reading Report notes, "[a]cross gender and age, choice rules. A majority of kids (89%) agree their favorite books are the ones that they have picked out themselves." Students need some guidance and scaffolding about how to make the right choices for themselves as readers, so help them become familiar with the various sections of their collections on- and offline, and ensure that all students know where to find the texts they seek.

Structured independent reading should be purposeful and directly linked to instruction. Each day, help students engage in their reading with clear expectations about the work they should do. What was the point made in the lesson? Was it a process lesson that taught the behaviors of real readers? Was it a strategy lesson that provided students with a specific reading strategy? Or was it a lesson rooted in content from academic standards? The independent reading should provide students with the opportunity to practice the skills that were addressed in their instruction.

Mr. Sanchez was in the middle of a unit of study on finding life lessons in novels. He demonstrated how readers notice when a character changes in some significant way in order to identify the life lesson that may be present in the book. He asked his class to find examples of characters who have changed in other books. He told his class that in today's independent reading, they should each read a story and notice when the main character changes and see if this reveals one of the life lessons in the story. Some students used sticky notes and others used their tech devices to jot notes about their thoughts as they read. Later, Mr. Sanchez brought the students back together to discuss their ideas about the life lessons they discovered in their stories.

Independent reading should be a time of active, accountable learning for both teacher and students, as everyone works together to build engagement, motivation, and dynamic academic achievement. Strong independent readers will curate their own ever-growing, ever-changing reading collections. They will show interest in learning new words and phrases, building their reading stamina as they become lost in the world of their texts. Strong independent readers discuss their own reading and actively listen to the ideas of other readers. They generate high-level inquiry questions and answer inferential questions with textual evidence. Strong independent readers are super readers.

What do students do during structured independent reading?

- Choose from a selection of high-interest texts.
- Read, read, read!
- Practice skills they are learning as a whole class.
- May connect thinking/discussion to shared ideas from a whole-class reading.
- Participate in conversations with partners about central ideas or shared texts.

Recommended Minimum Minutes for Daily Independent Reading*	
Grade	**Minutes**
K	10
1	15
2	20
3	25
4	30
5	30
6–8	20–30 given the constraints of a middle school schedule

*These are approximations. Use your judgment based on what you know about your students.

Readers make wise book choices. Reading can feel like riding a bike. Books can feel:
- uphill - a little bit hard
- level - a smooth ride, not too easy, not too hard
- downhill - a little bit easy

Readers Have Good Habits
- They choose books they like to read.
- They take care of books.
- They use 1 inch voices.
- They keep reading until time is up.

What do teachers do during structured independent reading time?

- Confer with individual students to further their skills.

- Help students who are having difficulty with phonics and phonemic strategies to practice their skills.

- Help students challenged by comprehension and fluency issues to practice under your watchful care and guidance.

- Coach discussions students are having in a partner talk.

- Help students choose books or other texts for their independent reading plans.

- Instruct small groups of students with similar challenges and strengths.

- Gather formative assessment data.

Taking a close look at the 7 Strengths helps us organize goals for structured independent reading:

Strength	In a 7 Strengths Classroom...
Belonging	Students work together to create a reading community to explore a world of knowledge and a diverse body of literature.
Friendship	Students bond through shared reading passions, building identity as readers, and working collaboratively.
Kindness	Students support one another across reading levels, working together to reach new dimensions as readers.
Curiosity	Students feed their curious minds by having a chance to select their own reading materials and ask and answer questions to pursue their genuine wonderings.
Confidence	Students practice reading at uphill levels (more challenging), downhill levels (less challenging), and smooth levels, making their own choices based on interest, passion, and purpose.
Courage	Students see challenge as part of the reading process and work through the hard parts with fortitude, perseverance, and determination.
Hope	Students set goals for themselves as readers, and set goals for how reading can change their lives and the lives of others.

Why should structured independent reading connect deeply to explicit instruction?

The connection between explicit instruction in reading and what students practice during structured independent reading time is the cornerstone of effective instruction. Students must be taught essential skills and strategies and be given time to apply what they have learned. That way, they develop the reading capacities that curricular standards demand of them. It is not sufficient for students to simply be sent off to "free read." Unstructured reading time and practices such as D.E.A.R. have benefits, but they don't provide the focused practice that most students need to stay engaged and learn what they need to learn.

Connect what you model during a lesson and what students practice during subsequent structured independent reading time. For example, you may use a sample informational text to model how readers use headings to determine what a part of the text will be about. Then, students would read informational texts independently for a large portion of the class period, paying attention to how the headings are helping them. They might have to highlight a couple of headings they found and be prepared to describe how they used the headings. These results may be shared in student notes for the teacher to see and/or during a whole-class discussion at the end of the period.

A Word About Stamina

Stamina is a sometimes underrated, yet crucial, element of how super readers build their muscles. As with sports, the athlete builds capacity by building minutes. Every minute added to the practice, every breath taken, makes the athlete stronger. Call attention to stamina-building in your classroom of super readers. Honor it, value it, and affirm it.

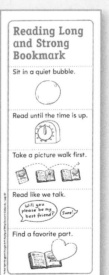

Reading Long and Strong Bookmark

Sit in a quiet bubble.

Read until the time is up.

Take a picture walk first.

Read like we talk.

Will you please be my best friend? Sure!

Find a favorite part.

Resource 5.11 (Grade K)

Reading Long and Strong Bookmark

Read until the time is up.

Make sure most books are on your level.

Choose an interesting book

Choose books from different genres.

Take a picture walk first.

Find a favorite part.

Resource 5.12 (Grade 1)

You may be reading aloud from *Confetti Girl* by Diana López as a whole-class instructional text, looking closely at the connection between characters and theme. The students may then be invited to look for similar connections from character to theme in their own independent reading texts. In this way, students are engaged in structured practice that reflects back to the whole-class lesson, but they are practicing in a text that makes the most sense for them.

One-to-One Reading Conversations/Conferring

What Is It? A focused conversation between a teacher and a student that explores the student's thinking and conclusions about a text, and possible strategies to enhance understanding and engagement during structured reading time.

Why Are Reading Conversations Helpful to Super Readers? The standards, research of best practices, and demands of college and career all point to more of an inquiry-based approach to how students learn to talk about books. It is important, therefore, that we create time each day to talk one-to-one with students about their reading lives during structured independent reading. These conversations should feature a great

Strength	Questions to Ask While Conferring With Students
Belonging	• How do you connect to the world of this story? • How did you reach out to someone as a reader today or this week?
Friendship	• Was there a way you listened deeply to another reader today? • How can our classmates be better reading friends toward each other?
Kindness	• How did you help someone as a learner today? • Is there a character who has taught you a lesson about kindness?
Curiosity	• What are you wondering about? • What are you learning about?
Confidence	• How are you building reading skills, including phonics and comprehension? • What did you read today that made you feel like a more confident person overall?
Courage	• How did you share in discussion today in a way that felt brave? • What did you try in your reading that felt brave?
Hope	• What are your goals for yourself as a reader? • What is your dream for yourself as a reader?

deal of active listening from adults. In fact, active listening will help us to be the best advocates and champions of super readers we can be. (See page 184 for a conferring checklist to use to assess students.)

We can invite students—even the youngest ones—to use the 7 Strengths by asking them the questions below when we confer with them.

Writing About Reading

What Is It? Students engage in writing in response to a text, which allows them to articulate and process their thinking or share their thinking with a wider audience.

Why Is Writing About Reading Helpful to Super Readers? Writing about reading can deepen the reading experience. Used wisely and with exceedingly good judgment, it can truly enhance a child's experience with text. We have identified five major categories:

Analytical writing: Students can write book reviews, literary essays, character sketches, and author profiles. These can be written in response to any reading genre.

Creative writing: Students can craft original, creative literary responses, such as a poem, an alternate ending, an interview, or a play inspired by the reading.

Critical insights: Students can draw critical insights to question or interrogate texts where they may see a bias present that troubles some conclusions that the text has drawn.

Self-evaluative writing: Students can self-evaluate to identify reading preferences, set goals, and reflect on strategy use and general growth as a reader.

Extension writing: Students can also tap into their curiosity and use the text as a springboard to inquiry and further research about a topic or theme they have found compelling. Perhaps a story about a historical character has inspired them to do their own historical research on their family or community. Or maybe a story that deals with science or technology has inspired them to conduct their own scientific investigations. Or they can have fun with modeling their responses around the genre of social media, trying to convey a response in a limited amount of characters.

Supporting Striving Readers

The following strategies are helpful to all students, but most particularly to striving readers:

- Focus on the positive.
- Value high-level thinking with lower-level text.

- Think about genres, authors, text type, environment, and other factors to *spark motivation*.

- Build stamina with multiple texts (instead of just one) during independent reading time.

- Model the following reading strategies:

  - Sound out the words and embrace phonics strategies.

  - Chunk the word (look for shorter words within longer words).

  - Skip the word (return to it later).

  - Flip the vowel sound.

- Use technology to increase student engagement and ease of response.

Supporting Emerging Bilinguals

The following strategies are helpful to all students, but most particularly to emerging bilinguals:

- Partner wisely. Make sure students have a variety of partners to turn and talk to so they can practice developing English skills with many different kinds of speakers and listeners. Create flexible reading partnerships so emerging bilinguals can work with other emerging bilinguals and also with native English speakers.

- Read aloud every day. Expose emerging bilinguals to new English grammar and vocabulary.

- Use visuals. As you read aloud, be sure students can clearly see the images on the pages. If possible, display images on the wall or screen, using a digital projector. Value students' interpretation of the art and the photographs—it's all part of reading development.

- Celebrate progress. When learning a language, students often make very wise errors based on what they know about their native language. Praise and point this out when you see that happening. For example, a child who puts an adjective after a noun instead of before it who is a native Spanish speaker is making a very logical choice.

- Encourage rereading. Emerging bilinguals need abundant opportunities to revisit text. Rereading a text or revisiting a familiar text helps to reinforce language structures and new vocabulary for a child. Have partners reread read-alouds to each other. Celebrate rereading of familiar texts.

- Honor students reading at all levels. Promote their oral language and critical thinking by inviting them to talk critically about lower-level texts.

- Make conversations matter. Help emerging bilinguals develop their oral communication skills by modeling conversational turns, such as: "I'd like to add to what you are saying." "I'd like to build off what _____ said." "I am wondering about what you said." Put those turns on a chart for students' reference.

- Treat writing as thinking. Recognize that writing can be a way for students to express themselves fully and more confidently. Provide them with sticky notes, index cards, and technology options; have them "think off the texts"; and use their notes when they speak aloud.

- Create word banks. Focus on academic language and words that trigger longer, complex oral thought, such as "however" and "in addition."

- Ensure library collections and online offerings include books in students' home languages.

This chapter highlighted the importance of structured independent reading as a central feature of instruction to build super readers. In the next chapter, we will share techniques for management of a classroom of independent, diverse super readers.

CHAPTER 12

MANAGEMENT STRATEGIES FOR THE SUPER READER CLASSROOM

Your classroom is an abundance of human life and spirit. And as wonderful as this can be, it's a feat of management every day, so we affirm you! Having multitudes of readers in your room (or online with you) means you are managing personalities and preferences, as well as varying experience levels. It can be exciting but also daunting. Here follows some of our favorite ways to keep the lively nature of a super reader classroom strong while creating peace and well-being for everyone inhabiting these spaces together.

Strategies to Promote Active Engagement for All Students

Turn and Talk

During a lesson, teachers may prompt students to turn to a partner and engage in a quick conversation to answer a question or share thoughts about a text. This can happen virtually, too. Students can turn and talk with signals on a chat bar or in the technologies you already use in class to have partners work together. When we ask students to turn and talk, they are able to practice a skill, strategy, or behavior while you listen in to assess understanding and offer your assistance. Give students a couple of minutes to talk with a partner. Make sure the "Turn and Talk" partnerships change often to give students a chance to talk with a variety of peers.

Stop and Jot

A Stop and Jot gives students a chance to quickly record their thinking in writing to develop and gauge their understanding of a topic. By asking a meaningful question and having students jot their response, you allow students the opportunity to demonstrate their understanding, identify any confusions, and develop their critical-thinking skills. This can also be done using technology, of course. The main idea here is that we don't take too much time: we invite our students to take two minutes to "Stop and Jot" to enliven their thinking in response to a text, especially during a read-aloud.

Strategies to Control Noise Level

Quiet Bubble

We can't expect young children to be completely silent as they read and write. However, we can create a buzz that feels comfortable for everyone—one that allows students to focus on their work. One way to do that is with a Quiet Bubble. When students are working, tell them to imagine that they are each reading or writing in a giant bubble of peaceful quiet. Loud voices will pop the bubble. The same holds true in the virtual environment. When students are meeting via their digital devices, they can use "Quiet Bubble" to allow one person at a time to offer a reflection.

Find these forms at scholastic.com /superreaderresources.

One-Inch Voice

The term "one-inch voice" is also extremely helpful. Our students understand the visual of one inch, and they can show you with their finger and thumb precisely how big that is. It helps them to have a visual because when adults say "Be quiet!" children often think they are being quiet!

A reminder of the one-inch voice helps them to visualize just what you mean by *quiet*. At the same time, we can also encourage voices to go beyond one inch. For example, when we are texting or writing to another person on a shared doc, sometimes the quieter voices stay very quiet. So we can also use this analogy to invite our students to be sure to include others in dialogue, wherever it's happening. We can say, "Let's get to a one-inch voice to help others have more inches in theirs."

Silent Motions

To encourage active listening and a strong sense of community, teach students to use hand signals. If a child has a question, she can raise two fingers together (index and middle) to let the speaker know that when she is finished, she has something to add. If students want to express that they feel the same way about what another person is describing, or have had the same experience, they can use the "me too" hand signal: making a fist, but holding out their pinkies and thumbs. Students then move their hands back and forth with their thumbs facing inward. Another hand signal you can use is "spirit fingers." When students appreciate others, they can hold their hands up next to their shoulders with their palms facing out and fingers pointed up, and wiggle their fingers.

You can also use thumbs up/thumbs down as a quick assessment for understanding of instructions and/or concept. Nonverbal signals allow teachers to keep the flow of the lesson moving forward. If we are in a virtual space, we can use emojis to indicate similar emotions or signs of support for someone else's ideas as a super reader. You can decide as a class which emojis will represent different actions and emotions around super reading.

Strategies to Manage Partner and Group Work

A and B Partners

Before asking students to work in pairs, plan who will be in each partnership. Once you have done that, make one partner the A partner and one the B partner. (You may also use colors, numbers, shapes, and so on, to designate the different roles in the partnership.) Then you can easily refer to the partners to give directions. For example:

> *Gather with partners. A's should sit on the side closest to the window. Turn to your partner and answer the question at hand. B's answer first, then A's. Today B's will read aloud to A's.*

Clock Buddies

Clock Buddies is a great tool for managing partner work in reading. Students get to set up their own partnerships using the simple clock visual, in which the hours of the clock identify a different partner. At the beginning of the school year, instruct students to select a partner for each blank slot on their clock. Circulate around the classroom to help ensure that both partners copy their names in the appropriate lines. Once the pairings are established you can assign tasks, like partner reading or share-outs. For example, "Today, you will be buddy reading with your 3 o'clock partner." This strategy helps promote engagement and collaboration between different students in a class.

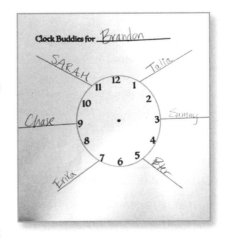

5 Ways to Recognize Hard Work

1. **Call-Out** During independent reading or writing practice, request a quick call-out. During the call-out, when you have students' attention, highlight a specific student as an example of hard work. "I love how Sarah helped her partner solve a challenging definition."

2. **7 Strengths Awards** Provide awards centered around the 7 Strengths. For example, the Curiosity Award can be given to a student who asks a question that leads to an interesting discussion.

3. **Shooting Stars** Send "shooting stars" to a student who took any kind of step, large or small, as a reader. Pantomime throwing a handful of sparkling stars at students while encouraging them to "catch" them.

4. **Snap Claps** Have the class or a small group give a student a round of "snap claps" (rapid finger snapping) for a quick and quiet way to affirm hard work.

5. **Partner Awards** Affirm the work reading partners do together by giving weekly awards to partnerships working in fellowship online or offline, for partnerships where one partner is truly advocating for another, or where the two partners have had breakthroughs as super readers (small and large).

Available at scholastic.com/superreaderresources.

Strategies to Facilitate Transitions

Student Call-and-Response

Engage students in rousing call-and-response chants at key points during the day.

Student: *Ready to read? (Clap, clap)*

Class: *Ready to read! (Clap, clap)*

Student: *Get what you need! (Clap, clap)*

Class: *Get what we need! (Clap, clap)*

Student: *Sit in your nook! (Clap, clap)*

Class: *Find your book! (Clap, clap)*

Student: *Ready to go! (Clap, clap)*

Class: *Ready to go! (Clap, clap)*

Musical Transitions

Use a specific song or musical instrument to signal to students when it is time to transition from one activity to another. For example, play a soothing song to let students know when independent reading is coming to a close, or a peppy song when it is time for students to choose books from the classroom library. Students quickly learn to associate the song with the segment of the lesson or the activity and smoothly transition.

> **READERS' SONG**
> **(to the tune of "Twinkle, Twinkle, Little Star")**
>
> We know when we hear
> this rhyme
> It's our song for Reading Time.
> Reading love is in my heart
> Everyone will do their part.
> Check the chart for
> where to go
> Reading Time, I love you so!

Tech Transitions

It's a fast-moving world when it comes to the developments of new technologies to support our work in creating super reader environments. If we are online with our students, or using technology to help us with transitions in the room, let's remember to create the human dimension no matter what. Be sure to check in with your students: "How is this feeling? How can the tech tools we use help us to gain more understanding of each other and help us get ready for the next part of our learning that is coming?" We can use the layered technology tools we have to do everything from alerting our students when it's time to make a change, to helping our students recognize when someone else might be having trouble.

Station Rotation: Create a station rotation that offers both an adaptive learning software as well as a teacher-led station. This cross-curricular, ELA-friendly classroom management strategy offers students the opportunity to use an online learning tool and gives teachers data as students learn, but avoids screen fatigue, as students have time to read with a teacher in the teacher-led portion.

Differentiating Reading Instruction: Set up a space online where students can log in at a time that works for them and their families. With this self-paced or asynchronous option, students can share responses to prompts or give book recommendations.

Digital Choice Boards: Similar to an old-school bingo board, these activity boards can be found online or created in a document that allows for hyperlinks. Students click through the activity board, filling it out throughout the week as they complete each activity.

(Monica Burns, 2021)

Helping Students Work on Their Own

Luckily, technology has arrived to help us a lot in this area. There are so many ways our students can use technology to communicate with one another as readers, sharing ideas and having fun making videos or slide decks of their reading experiences together. So working alone never has to be fully alone. Yet there are times when you want your students to be doing work around structured independent reading or practicing something as a super reader alone and you need them to be able to do these things without you while you help others.

It is helpful to make sure you set intentions with your students and practice with them what they can do if they need you while you are busy with something else. Review with them the importance of rereading (with texts they feel safe and happy with), as this builds stamina and will alleviate whatever is concerning them at that moment. Show them how to use super reading partners to ask questions online or offline. Share with them a conference sign-up sheet online or offline that they can use to make an appointment with you for a one-to-one. Just knowing they will soon be able to run something by you is enough to take the edge off an immediacy of need. And finally, celebrate and affirm when you see a student pushing through the hard parts on her own. Every day is an opportunity to make the most of the steps you see in your super readers becoming more confident and more independent.

Tech Tips

1. Introduce new tech tools to a small group of students and let them become the "experts" before a whole-class lesson.
2. Create instructions with screenshots to leave at stations where students will work in partners or independently.
3. Label student devices with names and numbers using colorful tape or stickers.

Strategies for Helping Students Stay Focused and Engaged

Every classroom has students who have a more difficult time staying on task and engaging fully 100 percent of the time in the planned activities. Consider the following three strategies:

Make learning tools accessible and readily available.

Make sure the classroom library or online texts students need to carry out expected tasks are accessible and well-organized. If you want students to write about their reading easily and fluidly, give them baskets of sticky notes, personalized notebooks, and tablets and other digital devices to reach for on their own.

Make routines familiar—but if they are not working, be empowered to change them.

The super reader classroom should feel predictable in its routines. Protect independent reading time each and every day (whether you are virtual or in person). The whole/small-one-to-one/whole model is a beautiful rhythm for a super reader classroom. But if it feels like you see your students' attention waver, or the time seems too long for them to read independently, pull back and bring the team together for a "7 Strengths Regroup." Invite the conversation (at every age!) by asking: "What's not working? What's getting in your way? What can I do to help remove the obstacles?"

Communicate clear expectations for daily reading work.

Posting anchor charts or keeping online records can help students remember and keep focused on the expectations. You can create a folder with pictures of anchor charts students can access on their laptops or a QR code they scan with a tablet that connects to an online resource for extra help.

Walking into a classroom of super readers can be deceiving. A sense of calm, students on task, a busy hum—these classrooms almost seem to run on their own. The trained eye, however, can see the amount of teaching and foundational work that went into creating a super reader environment, where every member of the community is engaged and learning. These management strategies will help you create such an environment, a joyfully trusting community in which every child is a super reader.

Next Steps

Next, we will share with you formative assessment tools that will help you see your students in all the ways they grow as readers and teach in ways that are deeply supportive of their growth: a strengths-based approach to how we observe and reflect upon student progress.

CHAPTER 13

ASSESSMENT TOOLS FOR THE SUPER READER CLASSROOM

I n this chapter, we share with you some innovative ways to assess your students formatively on their journeys to becoming super readers.

7 Strengths Student Survey

The 7 Strengths Student Survey allows you to learn detailed information about the child's opinion of him- or herself as a reader.

7 Strengths Checklist for Digital Citizenship

Engaging online is exciting and complex. This checklist assures that your students are giving and receiving information online thoughtfully and caringly.

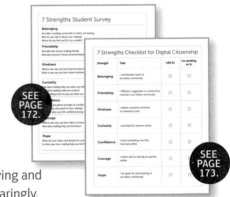

7 Strengths Rubric

The 7 Strengths Rubric helps you assess the intrinsic connection between your students' well-being and their academic literacy achievement. Add the number of checked boxes horizontally to determine proficiency in each strength. Add the number of checked boxes vertically to determine proficiency literacy in each literacy strand: reading, writing, listening, and speaking.

Super Reader Rubric

The Super Reader Rubric enables you to keep a running observational record of many super reading skills. It is based on an asset model, so it will help guide you to notice those skills your students can already do so that you can plan next goals and next steps for them.

Strength-Specific Goal-Setting Sheets

After you've gathered data on your super readers using the tools described thus far, use the goal-setting sheets to inform your instructional planning and differentiate instruction for every super reader. Analyze your data, looking for patterns of learning behavior and areas of need. Then work together to identify goals for each student for each strength.

Goal-Tracking Checklist

The Goal-Tracking Checklist can help you record goals for your super readers and the progress they have made toward mastery.

7 Strengths Conferring Checklist

Conferring is the best possible formative assessment there is. You can delve into the nuances of each student's reading progress. You can help your students set reading goals. The 7 Strengths Conferring Checklist helps you do all this.

Super Reader Log

A reading log can be a useful assessment and accountability tool as you manage your super readers' independence. Students can fill out the Super Reader Log regularly as they engage in the reading routines and work in the classroom, after school, and at home. The Super Reader Log is a twist on the traditional reading log because it infuses the 7 Strengths into the reading work.

These assessment tools are intended to be used to inform your teaching. (Find digital versions at scholastic.com/superreaderresources.) Observe your students and record your impressions. Seek the opinions of your students as well. Then analyze the information you gather to set goals for each child. Track your students' progress toward their goals and the extent to which they are growing into the super readers you know they can become.

7 Strengths Student Survey

Belonging

Describe a reading community to which you belong.
Who do you talk to about your reading?
Where do you feel you fit in as a reader?

Friendship

Describe one of your reading friends.
Describe someone whose recommendations you admire as a reader.

Kindness

What is one way you have learned about kindness through reading?
What is one way you have shown kindness to a fellow reader?

Curiosity

How does reading help you when you feel curious about something?
How does reading make you curious?
What reading tools do you use when you want to find out about something?

Confidence

How have you grown stronger as a reader?
What makes you proud of your reading?
Describe when you felt confident during reading time.

Courage

What is one way you have taken a chance as a reader?
How does reading help you feel brave?
When have you shared your ideas about your reading in a way that feels courageous for you?

Hope

What are your hopes and dreams for yourself as a reader?
In what ways does reading help you feel hopeful?

7 Strengths Checklist for Digital Citizenship

Strength	Task	I did it!	I'm working on it.
Belonging	I contributed a post to an online community.	☐	☐
Friendship	I offered a suggestion or constructive criticism in an online community.	☐	☐
Kindness	I added a positive comment to someone's post.	☐	☐
Curiosity	I searched for answers online.	☐	☐
Confidence	I tried something new that I learned online.	☐	☐
Courage	I took a risk by sharing an opinion online.	☐	☐
Hope	I set goals for participating in an online community.	☐	☐

7 Strengths Rubric

STRENGTH PROFICIENCY (horizontal tally)	
EMERGING (1–4 checks)	Beginning to show evidence of the skills and habits of the strength.
APPROACHING (5–8 checks)	Sometimes demonstrates evidence of the skills and habits of the strength.
ACHIEVING (9–12 checks)	Displays consistency in skills and habits associated with the strength.

	Reading	Writing	Listening	Speaking	SCORE
Belonging **Being a valued, cherished member of a larger community** Literacy and belonging connect by providing examples of community, cultivating safe space and common ground, and providing ways to identify, create, and share experiences of community.	☐ Finds connections between words and families of words ☐ Connects with others through shared experiences in reading ☐ Identifies with characters in books ☐ Connects communities in text to their own experiences	☐ Connects with others through shared writing experiences ☐ Connects to favorite authors ☐ Shares one's own community experience in writing	☐ Connects with others through shared experiences in conversation ☐ Demonstrates active engagement with others' ideas ☐ Demonstrates an understanding of the values of the group	☐ Expresses opinions in a community discussion ☐ Expresses perspectives that will further the learning of the community ☐ Uses ideas to verbally connect with others	
Friendship **Having close, trusting relationships and personal connections to others** Literacy builds friendship by providing examples of trusting relationships and allowing opportunities to explore multiple perspectives.	☐ Feels comfortable decoding words and exploring unfamiliar vocabulary with partners ☐ Shares texts with others ☐ Shares ideas with others based on reading and writing experiences ☐ Identifies qualities of connectedness/ friendship in books read	☐ Shares writing with others ☐ Creates connections between characters in one's own writing ☐ Connects to others as writers, finding commonalities in theme, topic, and craft	☐ Listens to stories and writing of others ☐ Invites others to share ideas to improve writing ☐ Shares thoughts about others' writing humbly and with appreciation	☐ Shares ideas with others in a give-and-take ☐ Shares ideas comfortably with others ☐ Reaches out to help friends share their ideas through extension of conversation or inquiry-based conference	
Kindness **Being compassionate toward others; expressing tenderness that has an impact, near and far** Literacy helps establish the language of kindness in both word and action by enabling practice forums for cultivating empathy and building bridges.	☐ Cares about characters and events in books ☐ Cares about the ideas of other readers in the room ☐ Cares about fellow readers in the community, creating an environment where all feel at ease ☐ Shows a sense of understanding for one's own stumbles and progress navigating difficult texts	☐ Shows interest in others' writing ideas ☐ Shows empathy in characters and plot ☐ Helps improve others' writing with care and tenderness	☐ Shares open-ended questions to demonstrate active listening ☐ Uses positive body language to demonstrate openness ☐ Affirms others' ideas in nonverbal ways	☐ Speaks about one's ideas in ways that incorporate values from books read together ☐ Expresses opinions with openness for others to add on ☐ Expresses ideas with care and tact, walking peers through one's thinking	
Curiosity **Fostering a willingness to explore new territory and test new theories** Literacy builds curiosity by inspiring questions, providing access to information, and offering an outlet for sharing ideas with the world.	☐ Explores words and ideas in text ☐ Explores different genres and styles of text ☐ Explores wonderings across texts	☐ Explores a variety of writing styles ☐ Explores use of author's craft ☐ Explores own passions and makes choices about what to write about	☐ Reacts to read-alouds with further inquiry ☐ Demonstrates openness to others' points of view ☐ Asks inquiring questions of others' reactions to text	☐ Explores ideas by talking about them ☐ Expresses ideas in the form of open-ended questions ☐ Shares plans for pursuing wonderings	

EMERGING: 1–4 • APPROACHING: 5–8 • ACHIEVING: 9–12

	Reading	Writing	Listening	Speaking	SCORE
Confidence **Thinking independently, expressing ideas, and pushing through the hard parts with resilience** Literacy builds confidence by enabling infinite worlds for exploration. The manipulation of language itself provides opportunity for creativity and stepping outside of oneself.	☐ Builds a diverse reading profile by reading books in various different genres ☐ Takes risks in reading, pushing through hard parts ☐ Builds skills by experimenting with different reading strategies ☐ Tries out new ways to break down words and use phonics and morphology to explore new language	☐ Experiments with new writing styles ☐ Builds new vocabulary ☐ Takes risks by trying new genres and examples of authors	☐ Listens without judging others ☐ Uses advice from peers or teacher to improve writing ☐ Builds skills by using active body language to indicate powerful listening	☐ Builds skills in speaking in public about one's ideas ☐ Builds strength in sharing opinions about books ☐ Builds capacity for sharing ideas that may not be the same as others'	
Courage **Having the strength to stand up for yourself, for others, and to take action when it is needed** Literacy builds courage by providing examples of courage both big and small. The development of literacy skills allows for scaffolded victories and opportunities for celebrating new strengths.	☐ Tackles hard words and uses phonics and other skills to break through the hard parts of sentences ☐ Takes chances as a reader on books that feel hard ☐ Takes chances on books that may seem out of one's interest area ☐ Sees empowerment connections between one's life and the books one is reading	☐ Takes a chance with a new writing style ☐ Takes a chance with a new writing genre ☐ Writes about topics that may introduce controversy or that requires standing up for something	☐ Takes the chance to listen to a different point of view ☐ Works hard on being a deep listener to a peer ☐ Works hard to incorporate ideas that could change one's mind	☐ Shares new ideas aloud ☐ Adds onto a conversation even when it's not the majority opinion ☐ Is able to disagree forthrightly and without rancor to build new ideas	
Hope **Thinking optimistically and believing that today's efforts will produce good things in the future for yourself and the world** Literacy builds hope by providing examples of belonging, curiosity, friendship, kindness, confidence, and courage.	☐ Sets reading goals ☐ Contributes to the well-being of the reading community with optimism ☐ Uses ideas from reading to think about community and world issues	☐ Sets writing goals ☐ Uplifts the community with stories/writing that impacts others ☐ Considers ways that writing can effect change	☐ Sets listening goals ☐ Approaches listening to peers with a sense of optimism about the value of their ideas ☐ Uses someone else's ideas to help further a productive conversation	☐ Sets speaking goals ☐ Approaches speaking to peers with a sense of optimism about the value of sharing ideas ☐ Uses one's own ideas to help further a productive conversation	
LITERACY STRAND PROFICIENCY (vertical tally)					

EMERGING: 1–4 • APPROACHING: 5–8 • ACHIEVING: 9–12

EMERGING (1–7 checked boxes)
APPROACHING (8–12 checked boxes)
ACHIEVING (15–21 checked boxes)

Super Reader Rubric

	EMERGING	APPROACHING	ACHIEVING	EXCEEDING
	An emerging student is in the earliest stages of meeting the demands of the indicator. The student requires a large amount of scaffolding to be successful.	An approaching student demonstrates some success with the demands of the indicator. The student requires some scaffolding to be successful.	An achieving student demonstrates solid success with the demands of the indicator. The student exhibits independence and little or no scaffolding.	An exceeding student demonstrates exemplary success with the demands of the indicator. The student exhibits a high level of independence.
ENGAGEMENT AND ENJOYMENT	• Demonstrates emerging interest in reading. • Begins to connect read-alouds to his or her own ideas. • Begins to name favorite books. • Begins to read through pictures (and possibly some text) with interest. • Begins to choose books based on familiarity with or interest in topic. • Begins to offer opinions about books. • Begins to read by choice during free or choice time.	• Sometimes demonstrates interest in reading. • Connects read-alouds to his or her own ideas and conversations. • Names favorite books and/or passages or pictures from books. • Sometimes reads text or reads pictures with focus. • Sometimes chooses books based on familiarity with or interest in topic. • Offers occasional opinions about texts.	• Consistently demonstrates interest in reading. • Makes connections between read-alouds, independent reading, and conversations. • Names favorite books, authors, and genres. • Builds minutes of independent reading time. • Chooses books based on passions, interests, and favorite authors. • Offers opinions about texts.	• Demonstrates strong interest in reading. • Makes insightful connections between read-alouds, independent reading, and conversations; discusses the text's ideas, themes, and structures. • Shows excitement about favorite books, authors, and genres; revisits favorite texts. • Reads voraciously, is not easily distracted, and can quickly become "lost in the reading world." • Makes strong, well-informed reading choices based on passions and interests, favorite genres, and favorite authors. • Offers strong, well-informed opinions about texts and recommends books to others.

	EMERGING	APPROACHING	ACHIEVING	EXCEEDING
FLUENCY AND EXPRESSION	• Begins to decode words. • Demonstrates emerging ability to read text fluently. • Begins to read words in isolation. • Begins to read with some expression. • Begins to heed punctuation.	• Sometimes reads with decoding strategies. • Sometimes reads text fluently. • Sometimes reads with appropriate phrasing. • Sometimes reads with appropriate expression. • Sometimes heeds punctuation.	• Internalizes decoding strategies. • Consistently reads text fluently. • Often reads with appropriate phrasing. • Often reads with appropriate expression. • Often heeds punctuation.	• Demonstrates powerful skills in decoding. • Demonstrates strong ability to read text fluently. • Always reads with exemplary phrasing. • Always reads with expression that indicates deep understanding of text. • Always uses punctuation to improve fluency and expression.
FOCUS AND STAMINA	• Demonstrates emerging ability to focus on reading. • Begins to stick with a text for a sustained time period. • Begins to self-regulate while reading to stay focused. • Reads for a small number of the recommended minutes* for the grade level.	• Sometimes demonstrates ability to focus on reading. • Sometimes sticks with a text for a sustained period of time. • Sometimes self-regulates while reading to stay focused. • Reads for some of the recommended minutes* for the grade level.	• Consistently demonstrates ability to focus on reading. • Consistently sticks with a text for a sustained period of time. • Consistently self-regulates while reading to stay focused, tuning out distractions. • Reads for most of the recommended minutes* for the grade level.	• Demonstrates exemplary ability to remain focused on reading. • Always sticks with a text, often requesting more reading time. • Always self-regulates while reading to stay focused, tuning out distractions, and losing him- or herself in the text. • Reads for more than the recommended minutes* for the grade level.
COMPREHENSION AND CRITICAL THINKING	• Demonstrates emerging comprehension and analysis of text. • Begins to identify ideas in texts. • Begins to ask clarifying questions to comprehend texts. • Begins to make connections between texts and the real world.	• Sometimes comprehends and analyzes texts. • Sometimes expresses ideas about texts. • Sometimes asks clarifying questions to comprehend texts. • Sometimes makes connections between texts and the world.	• Consistently comprehends and analyzes texts. • Consistently expresses ideas about texts. • Consistently asks clarifying questions to comprehend texts. • Consistently makes connections between texts and the real world.	• Demonstrates strong ability to comprehend and analyze texts. • Articulates ideas about texts clearly and completely. • Regularly analyzes texts and asks clarifying questions to improve comprehension. • Regularly makes deep connections between texts and the real world.

COLLABORATION AND COMMUNITY BUILDING	EMERGING	APPROACHING	ACHIEVING	EXCEEDING
	• Demonstrates emerging speaking and listening skills in partner or whole-group discussions. • Begins to participate in turn and talks. • Begins to engage in partner contributions. • Begins to participate in group discussions. • Begins to apply basic listening skills to engage partners. • Begins to balance listening and speaking in partner discussions. • Begins to express ideas inspired by read-alouds.	• Sometimes speaks and listens in partner and whole-group discussions. • Shares during turn and talks. • Responds to partners' contributions. • Participates in group discussions. • Demonstrates active listening skills by expressing interest in the subject and responding to who's speaking. • Calibrates the balance of listening and speaking with a partner. • Shares ideas from read-alouds that help unify the community.	• Consistently speaks and listens in partner and whole-group discussions. • Consistently shares during turn and talks. • Responds to and builds on peers' contributions. • Participates in group discussions and enriches the conversation with his or her contributions. • Demonstrates active listening skills such as showing interest in the topic and engaging in the discussion; reiterating what a partner expresses; perhaps using sentence starters such as, "I want to add on to what you are saying…," "I appreciate what you are saying…," and "I'm wondering about…" • Calibrates the balance of listening and speaking with a partner and in whole group. • Shares ideas from read-alouds that help the community develop the 7 Strengths.	• Demonstrates exemplary speaking and listening skills in partner and whole-group discussions. • Shares during turn and talks; offers comments that enhance and deepen the conversation. • Responds to and builds on peers' contributions. • Participates in group discussions and enriches the conversation with his or her contributions; draws in peers by asking them questions. • Demonstrates active listening skills by leaning in and showing interest; continues discussions with comments such as, "I want to build off your idea…" and "I want to go back to what you said." • Calibrates the balance of speaking and listening with a partner and in whole group; actively listens and deepens speakers' ideas. • Shares ideas from read-alouds and related discussions to foster growth of the community's 7 Strengths.

	EMERGING	APPROACHING	ACHIEVING	EXCEEDING
GOAL-SETTING AND SELF-REFLECTION	• Shows emerging interest in identifying him- or herself as a reader, writer, speaker, listener, and learner. • Begins to connect to others as a reader, writer, and learner. • Begins to identify him- or herself as a reader. • Begins to set a basic goal for him- or herself as a reader, writer, and learner. • Begins to view his or her own literacy skills through the lens of 7 Strengths. • Begins to persevere when literacy work is challenging. • Begins to identify lessons in literature.	• Sometimes names qualities of him- or herself as a reader, writer, speaker, listener, and learner. • Sometimes connects to others as a fellow reader, writer, and learner. • Identifies self as a reader in contexts such as school. • Sets one goal for him- or herself as a literacy learner. • Views his or her own literacy skills through the lens of 7 Strengths; applies lessons learned through reading to frame ideas about him- or herself. • Perseveres when literacy work is challenging. • Identifies themes and lessons in literature.	• Consistently names qualities of him- or herself as a reader, writer, speaker, listener, and learner. • Often connects to others as a fellow reader, writer, and learner. • Identifies him- or herself as a reader; can name some reading preferences, strengths, and challenges. • Can set some goals for him- or herself as a literacy learner and identify ways to meet those goals. • Views his or her own literacy skills through the lens of the 7 Strengths; applies lessons learned through reading and discussion to his or her own growth. • Perseveres through challenging parts of reading, writing, speaking, and listening with self awareness; views challenges as opportunities for literacy growth. • Identifies themes and lessons in literature and ideas from discussion; may think about and hope for change and progress in the world.	• Names many qualities of him- or herself as a reader, writer, and learner. • Strongly connects to others as a fellow reader, writer, speaker, listener, and learner. • Identifies him- or herself as a reader; can speak with ease about reading preferences, strengths, and challenges. • Can set many goals for him- or herself as a literacy learner and lay out a plan to meet them; reflects on progress regularly. • Views his or her own literacy skills through the lens of the 7 Strengths; regularly applies lessons learned through reading and discussion to his or her own growth; regularly seeks opportunities to grow stronger. • Perseveres through challenging parts of reading, writing, speaking, and listening with self awareness; views challenges as opportunities for literacy growth; continuously gains new skills. • Uses themes and lessons in literature and ideas from discussion to think about and hope for change and progress in the world.

*Recommended independent reading minutes per grade level: K: 10 minutes or more; Grade 1: 15 minutes or more; Grade 2: 20 minutes or more; Grade 3: 25 minutes or more; Grade 4: 30 minutes or more; Grade 5: 30 minutes or more; Grades 6-8: between 20–30 depending on class time

Goal Setting: Belonging

Task	I did it!	I'm working on it.	Notes
I welcome others with a caring perspective and mindset.	☐	☐	
I ask questions and show interest in other people's ideas and thoughts.	☐	☐	
I am practicing my own feeling of comfort and well-being as a reader in the room.	☐	☐	
I share my thoughts and ideas in ways to help make my community strong.	☐	☐	
I support super reader routines that will help the entire community feel strong.	☐	☐	
I help to make change if something isn't working for us.	☐	☐	

Goal Setting: Friendship

Task	I did it!	I'm working on it.	Notes
I offer help when a friend needs it as a reader.	☐	☐	
I reach out to invite someone to join me in a book talk.	☐	☐	
I connect virtually with new friends as readers.	☐	☐	
I find themes in books that are about friendship and discuss these themes.	☐	☐	
I invite someone I may not know well or who may need a friend to be my reading partner.	☐	☐	
I listen to others' opinions and add on or disagree in ways that feel productive.	☐	☐	
I share book recommendations.	☐	☐	

Goal Setting: Kindness

Task	I did it!	I'm working on it.	Notes
I am kind to myself as a reader, not judging myself.	☐	☐	
I show care for others' ideas, not judging them.	☐	☐	
I am supportive of my classmates as they work on their skills.	☐	☐	
I respect other people's book choices and opinions about books.	☐	☐	
I am helpful and caring when someone else is struggling.	☐	☐	
I empathize with characters in stories.	☐	☐	
I am thinking about my role as a super reader in the world, and how I can be of help to others.	☐	☐	

Goal Setting: Curiosity

Task	I did it!	I'm working on it.	Notes
I ask questions about what I am reading.	☐	☐	
I ask questions of my peers about their ideas in a way that feels supportive.	☐	☐	
I seek understanding about what I am reading by questioning as I go.	☐	☐	
I further my inquiry by reading across multiple texts to find answers.	☐	☐	
I share wonderings that build off others' ideas.	☐	☐	
I share new wonderings that will help our community feel inspired.	☐	☐	

Goal Setting: Courage

Task	I did it!	I'm working on it.	Notes
I try to learn new words and push through hard parts of books I'm reading.	☐	☐	
I share ideas that may be new and that I am exploring.	☐	☐	
I speak out about my ideas, on- or offline.	☐	☐	
I listen deeply to ideas that may not always be aligned to mine.	☐	☐	
I consider ways reading makes me want to change the world and take action.	☐	☐	
I learn from stories how to be courageous in the world.	☐	☐	

Goal Setting: Confidence

Task	I did it!	I'm working on it.	Notes
I share my views about what we are reading.	☐	☐	
I read aloud to others.	☐	☐	
I invite others to share their ideas.	☐	☐	
I try out harder words and practice the hard parts of reading.	☐	☐	
I learn as I read and then use my learnings to inform my conversations.	☐	☐	
I listen with openness to other people's ideas.	☐	☐	

Goal Setting: Hope

Task	I did it!	I'm working on it.	Notes
I set goals for myself as a super reader.	☐	☐	
I connect with characters who have dreams and make my own.	☐	☐	
I listen to the hopes and dreams of others.	☐	☐	
I inspire others to have hope, even when there is struggle.	☐	☐	
I use my reading to consider and imagine ways we can change the world together.	☐	☐	

Goal-Tracking Checklist

Student Name:	Demonstrated Mastery	Working Toward Mastery	Requires Further Help	Next Steps (small-group work, conference, etc.)
Goal 1	☐	☐	☐	☐
Goal 2	☐	☐	☐	☐
Goal 3	☐	☐	☐	☐

7 Strengths Conferring Checklist

Student Name: _____   Date: _____

Strength	Observations	Next Steps
Belonging ☐ How are you feeling in this community? ☐ How are you welcoming others? ☐ How are you finding books that represent you/others?		
Friendship ☐ How are you reaching out to someone who needs a reading friend? ☐ How are you showing self-care as you read through hard parts? ☐ What themes are you finding in books that make you feel more connected to others? ☐ What would it take for you to feel really solid and social in this super reader classroom?		
Kindness ☐ How are you sharing well-being with others? ☐ How are you finding themes of care in books you are reading? ☐ How are you showing self-kindness when you are struggling?		
Curiosity ☐ How are you asking questions about what you are reading? ☐ How are you using questions to further your reading? ☐ How are you asking questions as you decode? Do your phonics strategies work well for you? What other strategies are you using? ☐ How are you finding out about new words?		

Strength	Observations	Next Steps
Confidence ☐ How are you growing in your phonics skills? ☐ How are you learning to tackle hard words? ☐ How are you becoming more confident in talking about theme and ideas in books? ☐ How are you working on sharing your ideas confidently with others? ☐ How are you reaching out to others to help? ☐ How are you building stamina as a reader?		
Courage ☐ How are you tackling the tough parts of reading? ☐ How are you showing courage as a super reader to try something new? ☐ How are you having the courage to share your ideas about what we are reading? ☐ How are you trying something new as a reader? ☐ How are you imagining yourself as a world changer based on what you are reading?		
Hope ☐ How are you setting goals for yourself as a super reader? ☐ How can I help you achieve those goals? ☐ How are you thinking big and dreaming big to accomplish big successes in your reading today, this month, this year? ☐ How are you reading in a way that makes you feel so strong that you could change the world? How can I help you do that?		

Super Reader Log

Name: _____ Date: _____

The 7 Strengths: Belonging, Friendship, Kindness, Curiosity, Confidence, Courage, and Hope

Title/Author	Type of Text	Stamina Meter	Engagement Meter	Enjoyment Meter
		① hard to keep going ② working on building minutes ③ read for full time	① not feeling very engaged ② feeling a little engaged ③ feeling somewhat engaged ④ feeling highly engaged	① didn't enjoy ② enjoyed a little bit ③ somewhat enjoyed ④ thoroughly enjoyed

When I read this text, I build the strength of _____ by

When I read this text, I build the strength of _____ by

When I read this text, I build the strength of _____ by

CHAPTER 14

PLANNING TOOLS FOR THE SUPER READER CLASSROOM

Building a community of super readers happens all day, every day, as we provide space and support during school and out-of-school time. The 7 Strengths can help us plan a solid and structured year for super readers. Think big picture first by making an overall plan for how the year should be laid out, and then think more specifically day by day, hour by hour. What follows are planning tools to help you in this work. (For downloadable versions of checklists and record-keeping forms, go to scholastic.com/superreaderresources.)

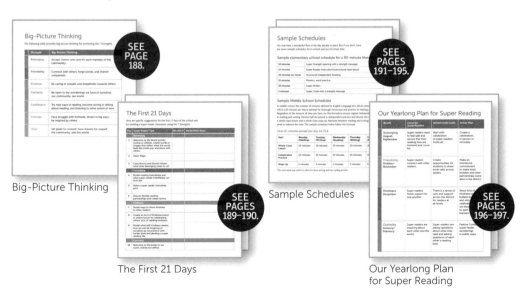

Big-Picture Thinking

The First 21 Days

Sample Schedules

Our Yearlong Plan for Super Reading

Big-Picture Thinking

The following table provides big-picture thinking for promoting the 7 Strengths.

Strength	Big-Picture Thinking
Belonging	Accept, honor, and care for each member of this community.
Friendship	Connect with others, forge bonds, and cherish uniqueness.
Kindness	Be caring of oneself, and empathetic toward others.
Curiosity	Be open to the wonderings we have of ourselves, our community, our world.
Confidence	Try new ways of reading, become strong in talking about reading, and listen to other points of view.
Courage	Face struggle with fortitude, dream in big ways, be inspired by others.
Hope	Set goals for oneself; have dreams for oneself, the community, and the world.

The First 21 Days

Here are specific suggestions for the first 21 days of the school year for building a Super Reader Classroom, using the 7 Strengths.

Day	Super Reader Task	We Did It!	Notes/Next Steps
	Belonging		
1	Welcome to My World activity (online or offline); create words or images that reflect what the world feels like inside you and share with others.		
2	Heart Maps		
3	Class Norms and Shared Values: What does belonging mean to us?		
	Friendship		
4	Model reading friendships and what super reader friendships can look like.		
5	Make a super reader friendship pact.		
6	Discuss flexible reading partnerships and create norms.		
	Kindness		
7	Model ways to show kindness to other readers.		
8	Create an Acts of Kindness board or online forum for celebrating others' acts of reading kindness.		
9	Model what self-kindness means: how we can be forgiving of ourselves as we practice with harder texts and develop a super reading life.		
	Curiosity		
10	Welcome to the books in our room, online and offline.		

Day	Super Reader Task	We Did It!	Notes/Next Steps
	Curiosity		
11	Set up a wondering wall, online or offline, for ongoing questions about books and life.		
12	Have rotating curiosity partners where super readers get to ask each other questions about their life, hopes, and dreams.		
	Confidence		
13	Model stamina-building by reading a variety of books during independent reading.		
14	Model how we can use technology and other tools to raise our own quiet voices.		
15	Model how to use reading strategies to push through hard parts.		
	Courage		
16	Model how we find courage in the characters we read about.		
17	Model how reading itself requires courage; reading hard books or new genres takes courage, and that we honor that.		
18	Model how we find inspiration in stories of all kinds and are constantly thinking about how we take small and big steps to support other people's courage, too.		
	Hope		
19	Make a super reader hopes and dreams chart, online or offline, for the entire class.		
20	Create self-goals for super reading.		
21	Model how reading leads us to our biggest hopes and dreams and create a Heart Map for Hopes and Dreams.		

Sample Schedules

You may have a wonderful flow of the day already in place. But if you don't, here are some sample schedules for in-school and out-of-school time.

Sample elementary school schedule for a 90-minute literacy block

10 minutes	Super Strength opening with a strength message
15 minutes	Super Reader instruction/instructional read-aloud
20 minutes (or more)	Structured independent reading
15 minutes	Phonics, word practice
25 minutes	Super Writers
5 minutes	Close with a strength message

Sample Middle School Schedules

In middle school, the number of minutes allotted for English Language Arts (ELA) varies significantly. 100 to 120 minutes per day is optimal for thorough instruction and practice in reading and writing. Regardless of the amount of time you have, try this formula to ensure regular independent practice in reading and writing: Devote half the period to independent practice and devote the other half to a whole-class lesson and a whole-class wrap-up. Alternate between reading and writing across the week to balance the time. The sample schedules below follow this formula.

One 50-minute period per day for ELA

Day*	Monday (Reading)	Tuesday (Writing)	Wednesday (Reading)	Thursday (Writing)	Friday (Reading)
Whole-Class Lesson	20 minutes	20 minutes	20 minutes	20 minutes	20 minutes
Independent Practice	25 minutes	25 minutes	25 minutes	25 minutes	25 minutes
Wrap-Up	5 minutes	5 minutes	5 minutes	5 minutes	5 minutes

*The next week may switch to allow for three writing and two reading periods.

Two 50-minute periods per day for ELA

		Monday	Tuesday	Wednesday	Thursday	Friday
50-minute period #1	**Whole-Class Reading Lesson**	20 minutes	20 minutes	20 minutes	20 minutes	20 minutes
	Structured Reading Practice	25 minutes	25 minutes	25 minutes	25 minutes	25 minutes
	Reading Wrap-Up	5 minutes	5 minutes	5 minutes	5 minutes	5 minutes
50-minute period # 2	**Whole-Class Writing Lesson**	20 minutes	20 minutes	20 minutes	20 minutes	20 minutes
	Structured Independent Writing Practice	25 minutes	25 minutes	25 minutes	25 minutes	25 minutes
	Writing Wrap-Up	5 minutes	5 minutes	5 minutes	5 minutes	5 minutes

Extended Day Program

Below is a schedule for an extended day program designed to nurture super readers.
There is plenty of time for reading together and independently, and sharing ideas with others.

3:00–3:10	Warm-Up
3:10–3:30	Workout in Reading and Writing
3:30–3:50	Structured Independent Practice
3:50–4:30	Homework Time
4:30–4:40	Cool Down and Wrap-Up

LitCamp Schedule

The 7 Strengths have been used as a powerful framework across the United States in the program LitCamp, created by LitWorld and Scholastic. Here is a sample schedule; timing is very flexible and easily adjusted depending on your district's needs.

Opening Campfire (15 mins)	• Greeting • Community-Building Activity • Transition Song • Words of the Day • Materials
Read-Aloud (25 mins)	• Interactive read-aloud with fiction or nonfiction text
Bring the Text to Life (20 mins)	• Activity with listening and speaking objectives
Reading Power (25 mins)	• Skills-based activities related to the read-aloud text
Bunk Time: Structured Reading (20 mins)	• Books chosen by campers
Community Lit (15 mins)	• Game or conversational activity
Writing Power (15 mins)	• Writing activity aligned with the read-aloud text
Closing Campfire (15 mins)	• Word game • Reflections • Praise and affirmations

7 Strengths Partnership Checklist

This checklist guides students to bring the 7 Strengths to their work with partners.

Task	I did it!	I'm working on it.	Notes
BELONGING: I greet my partner with a welcome.	☐	☐	
FRIENDSHIP: I share a connection with my partner when discussing books.	☐	☐	
KINDNESS: I am helpful and humble when working with my partner on the tough parts of reading.	☐	☐	
CURIOSITY: I ask questions about my partner's ideas that feel supportive.	☐	☐	
CONFIDENCE: I affirm my partner's small and big steps forward as a reader.	☐	☐	
COURAGE: I am brave in expressing ideas with my partner, and I am brave in hearing ideas that won't always match.	☐	☐	
HOPE: I set positive reading goals with my partner.	☐	☐	

Short-Term Goal Template: Use this template to help students set and meet short-term reading goals. Encourage them to be specific and to articulate how their goals will help them as readers.

Name:		Date:	I did it!
What will you do to become a stronger reader this week?			☐
What will you do to become a stronger reader this month?			☐
What kind of support might you need to become a stronger reader now?			☐

Long-Term Goal Guide: Use this guide to help students set long-term reading goals and to visualize specific ways to achieve them. Once goals are set, check progress and revise or set new goals as necessary.

Name:			Date:	
Reading Goal	**Target Date**	**How will I accomplish this goal?**	**Who can help me? How?**	**I did it!**
				☐
				☐
				☐
				☐
				☐

A Yearlong School/District Calendar for Super Reading

Month	Focus for Super Readers	School-wide Goals	Action Plan
Belonging **August/** **September**	Super readers need to feel safe and secure that their reading lives are honored and cared for.	Start with celebration of super readers. Invite all.	Create a celebration, in person or remotely.
Friendship **October/** **November**	Super readers connect with other readers.	Create opportunities for students to share book talks across grades.	Make an intentional commitment to make book buddies and other partnerships come alive in the district.
Kindness **December**	Super readers foster support for one another.	There is a sense of care and support across the district for readers at all levels.	Show Acts of Kindness on bulletin boards and virtually, celebrating how we show kindness to each other as learners.
Curiosity **January/** **February**	Super readers are inquiring about each other and the world.	Super readers are asking questions about what they read and asking questions of each other's reading lives.	Feature curious super reader wonderings in public ways.

Month	Focus for Super Readers	School-wide Goals	Action Plan
Confidence **March/April**	Super readers are taking new leaps!	Super readers are celebrating new steps in becoming super readers around decoding, comprehension, and more.	Celebrate Confidence with a Confidence Celebration.
Courage **May/June**	Super readers are fierce and brave in caring for their own reading lives, their community, and their world.	Super readers make a plan to take a step to helping others or to raising their own voices in response to what they are reading.	Create a Courage Role Model Display on- or offline where students of all ages can weigh in on what characters in books have meant to them.
Hope **July/August**	Super readers are making dreams come true.	Super readers are visibly creating hopes and dreams for self, community, and world.	LitCamp is on!

STRENGTHS FOR YOU

These past days, months, and years have been life-changing for all of us. We have learned how to cope with solitude, with the seismic shifts of a pandemic world, and, in spite of this, we have connected with our students and families across screens and distance. We have seen how reading and stories can bring us together and keep us learning and growing even when the world feels uncertain and fragile. As our book comes to an end, we are here with you to pay tribute to this work you do and to

invite you to continue to walk with us on this journey, even as the world changes yet again. Let these last pages be not an ending, but a beginning—for all of us. Remember what we said at the very beginning of this book: that reading is humankind's greatest innovation. In all the twists and turns of this ever-changing world, reading is a beacon and a guidepost, and we use it for many reasons, on many platforms. It accompanies us.

Let us together create spaces in which all our students can and will thrive as super readers, where they can go into the world ready for what may come next, the hard and the joyful. Let us fortify all our super readers with loving care, friendship-making, and kindness-creating, where every student becomes curious, confident, and courageous in their learning and growing. And let us believe in our work as big and transformational: in which, with the superpowers of super reading, every child has the gift of hopes and dreams that can, in fact, come true.

These strengths will accompany our students to a world they will inhabit long after we are gone. The strengths are not only about how we inspire readers; they are about how we inspire world changers. Our students are our precious gifts we have been given—a profound legacy we are leaving the world. Reading, writing, and learning together gives our students a chance to shine their brightest and live up to their greatest inner potential. They are our future leaders, teachers, engineers, electricians, artists, innovators, researchers, community members, neighbors, friends, and, yes, parents.

Your super reader work will live inside your students for the whole of their lives, for so many years to come. This child you teach now may grow up to teach his own child those same principles—remembering you, your voice, your affirmations, your spirit, inside of him.

Today, we accompany these wonderful students on their learning journey. Tomorrow, they will accompany someone else. Thank you for all you do, and have done to make the world a better place for all of them and the generations to come.

Let's keep going, together.

7 Strengths for You

A 7 Strengths-inspired wish for you, educators, to send you on your way:

Belonging		That you will find a sense of well-being in community with other educators, with your students, and with their families that uplifts you.
Friendship		That you will find connections to your students, to your colleagues, and to your community through the words and stories that inspire you all.
Kindness		That you will be kind to yourself on a hard day, kind to others every day, and find ways to emulate empathy in the books and stories you read.
Curiosity		That you will be inspired by your students' wonderings and your own inquiry and lifelong learning to be rejuvenated every day.
Confidence		That you will learn and grow in the work you do as an educator, and that you will take chances to try new things for the rest of your life.
Courage		That, in every day of this precious life of yours, you will find fearlessness, resilience, and inner strength to persevere, overcome, and transcend.
Hope		That you can dream your biggest hopes and dreams, that you cultivate dreams in others, and that through the work you do, we are all changed.

7 Strengths Children's Books

Here we have curated for you a strengths-specific collection. Authentic texts give children and young adults pathways to find themselves, connect to their communities, and build new worlds. We have worked side by side with children and young adults, teachers, parents, caregivers, and community members to shape a list that will accompany you in your teaching journey. Encourage your students to discover new titles to add to this collection and to debate over which book signals which strength. That is all part of the joy and the deep work of super reading: It is never finished, the conversation is ongoing, and the stories can sustain us in myriad ways. Here's to all the super reading you will do together! Please visit scholastic.com/superreaderresources for a digital version of this list, Spanish-language titles, and additional titles of interest and enjoyment.

STRENGTH ONE: BELONGING

Grades K–2

Alma and How She Got Her Name by Juana Martinez-Neal

Bigmama's by Donald Crews

A Birthday Basket for Tia by Pat Mora

Everything You Need for a Treehouse by Carter Higgins

Fresh Princess by Denene Millner

Hey, Wall: A Story of Art and Community by Susan Verde

Library Lion by Michelle Knudsen

My People by Langston Hughes

The New Small Person by Lauren Child

Planet Kindergarten by Sue Ganz-Schmitt

'Twas Nochebuena by Roseanne Greenfield Thong

Grades 3–5

Bud, Not Buddy by Christopher Paul Curtis

Carter Reads the Newspaper by Deborah Hopkinson

El Deafo by Cece Bell

Farmer Will Allen and the Growing Table by Jacqueline Briggs Martin

The Girl Who Thought in Pictures: The Story of Dr. Temple Grandin by Julia Finley Mosca

Hidden Figures: The True Story of Four Black Women and the Space Race by Margot Lee Shetterly

Immigrant Architect: Rafael Guastavino and the American Dream by Berta de Miguel and Kent Diebolt

Landed by Milly Lee

The Sound of All Things by Myron Uhlberg

Tar Beach by Faith Ringgold

Testing the Ice by Sharon Robinson

Grades 6–8

Drama by Raina Telgemeier

Fish in a Tree by Lynda Mullaly Hunt

Forest World by Margarita Engle

Garvey's Choice by Nikki Grimes

The House on Mango Street by Sandra Cisneros

The Lions of Little Rock by Kristin Levine

The Phantom Tollbooth by Norton Juster

They Call Me Güero: A Border Kid's Poems by David Bowles

Wonder by R. J. Palacio

STRENGTH TWO: FRIENDSHIP

Grades K–2

All Right Already! A Snowy Story by Jory John

Bee-Wigged by Cece Bell

Crazy Hair Day by Barney Saltzberg

How to Grow a Friend by Sara Gillingham

Madlenka by Peter Sís

Mango, Abuela, and Me by Meg Medina

Maria Had a Little Llama/María Tenía Una Llamita by Angela Dominquez

Maybe Tomorrow? by Charlotte Agell

One Cool Friend by Toni Buzzeo

Rita & Ralph's Rotten Day by Carmen Agra Deedy

Those Shoes by Maribeth Boelts

Yo! Yes? by Chris Raschka

Grades 3–5

Big Foot and Little Foot by Ellen Potter

Charlotte's Web by E. B. White

Dancing Home by Alma Flor Ada

Fenway and Hattie by Victoria J. Coe

The Junkyard Wonders by Patricia Polacco

The Madman of Piney Woods by Christopher Paul Curtis

The Other Side by Jacqueline Woodson

Owen & Mzee: The True Story of a Remarkable Friendship by Isabella Hatkoff, Craig Hatkoff, and Paula Kahumbu

True Tales of Animal Heroes by Allan Zullo

Wedgie & Gizmo by Suzanne Selfors

Grades 6–8

Catching a Story Fish by Janice N. Harrington

Drita: My Homegirl by Jenny Lombard

Duke by Kirby Larson

Holes by Louis Sachar

If a Tree Falls at Lunch Period by Gennifer Choldenko

The Kind of Friends We Used to Be by Frances O'Roark Dowell

Salt: A Story of Friendship in a Time of War by Helen Frost

The Season of Styx Malone by Kekla Magoon

Spin by Lamar Giles

A Touch of Ruckus by Ash Van Otterloo

STRENGTH THREE: KINDNESS

Grades K–2

Big Red Lollipop by Rukhsana Khan

A Bike Like Sergio's by Maribeth Boelts

Chrysanthemum by Kevin Henkes

Each Kindness by Jacqueline Woodson

Kindness to Share from A to Z by Peggy Snow and Todd Snow

Lucía the Luchadora and the Million Masks by Cynthia Leonor Garza

Mice and Beans by Pam Muñoz Ryan

Miss Rumphius by Barbara Cooney

We Are Grateful: Otsaliheliga by Traci Sorell

Wings by Christopher Myers

Grades 3–5

Addy's Cup of Sugar by Jon J Muth

Butterflies Belong Here: A Story of One Idea, Thirty Kids, and a World of Butterflies by Deborah Hopkinson

The Little Ships: The Heroic Rescue at Dunkirk in World War II by Louise Borden

Manjhi Moves a Mountain by Nancy Chrunin

Mufaro's Beautiful Daughters by John Steptoe

Saving Winslow by Sharon Creech

The Three Questions by Jon J Muth

The Trees of Dancing Goats by Patricia Polacco

Waiting for the Biblioburro by Monica Brown

Zen Shorts by Jon J Muth

Grades 6-8

The Camping Trip That Changed America by Barb Rosenstock

Freak the Mighty by Rodman Philbrick

Moo by Sharon Creech

Thirteen Ways of Looking at a Black Bo by Tony Medina

STRENGTH FOUR: CURIOSITY

Grades K–2

Abuela by Arthur Dorros

Boy, Were We Wrong About Dinosaurs! by Kathleen V. Kudlinski

Chameleons Are Cool by Martin Jenkins

The Day the Crayons Quit by Drew Daywalt

Hello, Ocean! by Pam Muñoz Ryan

The Little Red Fort by Brenda Maier

The Magician's Hat by Malcolm Mitchell

An Orange in January by Dianna Hutts Aston

Penguin Day: A Family Story by Nic Bishop

What If You Had Animal Hair? by Sandra Markle

The Word Collector by Peter H. Reynolds

Grades 3–5

Abe Lincoln's Dream by Lane Smith

Electrical Wizard: How Nikola Tesla Lit Up the World by Elizabeth Rusch

Grace Hopper: Queen of Computer Code by Laurie Wallmark

If Polar Bears Disappeared by Lily Williams

Layla and the Bots by Vicky Fang

River by Elisha Cooper

Sky Color by Peter H. Reynolds

Star Stuff: Carl Sagan and the Mysteries of the Cosmos by Stephanie Roth Sisson and Stephanie Sisson

The Sun Is Kind of a Big Deal by Nick Seluk

The Three Questions by Jon J Muth

Titanosaur: Discovering the World's Largest Dinosaur by Diego Pol and Jose Luis Carballido

Grades 6–8

The Dinosaurs of Waterhouse Hawkins by Barbara Kerley

The Evolution of Calpurnia Tate by Jacqueline Kelly

How to Be an Elephant: Growing Up in the African Wild by Katherine Roy

Who Wants Pizza? The Kids' Guide to the History, Science, & Culture of Food by Jan Thornhill

Wonders of the World by Toby Reynolds and Paul Calver

STRENGTH FIVE: CONFIDENCE

Grades K–2

All Because You Matter by Tami Charles

Chester the Brave by Audrey Penn

The Dot by Peter H. Reynolds

Ellie by Mike Wu

Even Superheroes Make Mistakes by Shelly Becker

Exclamation Mark by Amy Krouse Rosenthal

My Very Favorite Book in the Whole Wide World by Malcolm Mitchell

Niño Wrestles the World by Yuyi Morales

Standing on Her Shoulders by Monica Clark-Robinson

Unicorn Thinks He's Pretty Great by Bob Shea

Where Are You From? by Yamile Saied Méndez

Grades 3-5

Bobby the Brave (Sometimes) by Lisa Yee

Broken Bike Boy and the Queen of 33rd Street by Sharon G. Flake

Building Zaha: The Story of Architect Zaha Hadid by Victoria Tentler-Krylov

Doctor Esperanto and the Language of Hope by Mara Rockliff

Just Like Josh Gibson by Angela Johnson

Long Shot by Chris Paul

Looking Like Me by Walter Dean Myers

Planting Stories: The Life of Librarian and Storyteller Pura Belpré by Anika Aldamuy Denise

Saint Louis Armstrong Beach by Brenda Woods

When Marian Sang: The True Recital of Marian Anderson, The Voice of the Century by Pam Muñoz Ryan

Grades 6–8

Brown Girl Dreaming by Jacqueline Woodson

Favorite Greek Myths by Mary Pope Osborne

Finding Langston by Lesa Cline-Ransome

The Hunger Games by Suzanne Collins

The Love and Lies of Rukhsana Ali by Sabina Khan

Rebel Girls Lead: 20 Tales of Extraordinary Women by Elena Favilli and Francesca Cavallo

The Serpent's Secret by Sayantani DasGupta

Storm Thief by Chris Wooding

STRENGTH SIX: COURAGE

Grades K–2

Brave by Stacy McAnulty

Fire! Fuego! Brave Bomberos by Susan Middleton Elya

Gordon Parks by Carole Boston Weatherford

Gustavo the Shy Ghost by Flavia Z. Drago

Ish by Peter H. Reynolds

Jabari Jumps by Gaia Cornwall

Let's Play in the Forest While the Wolf Is Not Around by Claudia Rueda

School's First Day of School by Adam Rex

Sheila Rae, the Brave by Kevin Henkes

Stand Tall, Molly Lou Melon by Patty Lovell

Tiny T. Rex and the Very Dark Dark by Jonathan Stutzman

Grades 3–5

The Dreamer by Pam Muñoz Ryan

Granddaddy's Turn: A Journey to the Ballot Box by Michael S. Bandy and Eric Stein

The Hallelujah Flight by Phil Bildner

I Survived the Galveston Hurricane, 1900 by Lauren Tarshis

Interstellar Cinderella by Deborah Underwood

Memphis, Martin, and the Mountaintop: The Sanitation Strike of 1968 by Alice Faye Duncan

Moonshot: The Flight of Apollo 11 by Brian Floca

Nothing Stopped Sophie: The Story of Unshakable Mathematician Sophie Germain by Cheryl Bardoe

The Rooster Who Would Not Be Quiet! by Carmen Agra Deedy

Say Something by Peter H. Reynolds

Sojourner Truth's Step-Stomp Stride by Andrea Davis Pinkney

When Marian Sang by Pam Muñoz Ryan

Grades 6–8

Esperanza Rising by Pam Muñoz Ryan

Front Desk by Kelly Yang

Gaby, Lost and Found by Angela Cervantes

How I Became a Ghost by Tim Tingle

I Survived (Books 1–6) by Lauren Tarshis

Just Juice by Karen Hesse

Serafina and the Black Cloak by Robert Beatty

Shadowshaper by Daniel José Older

A Time to Dance by Padma Venkatraman

The Watsons Go to Birmingham—1963 by Christopher Paul Curtis

Yes! We Are Latinos by Alma Flor Ada and F. Isabel Campoy

STRENGTH SEVEN: HOPE

Grade K–2

ABC Mindful Me by Christiane Engel

Come On, Rain! by Karen Hesse

Eight Days: A Story of Haiti by Edwidge Danticat

Frida Kahlo and Her Animalitos by Monica Brown

Happy Birthday, Martin Luther King, Jr. by Jean Marzollo

Max Found Two Sticks by Brian Pinkney

Ruby's Wish by Shirin Yim Bridges

Steam Train, Dream Train by Sherri Duskey

Tía Isa Wants a Car by Meg Medina

What a Wonderful World by Bob Thiele and George David Weiss

Grades 3–5

Alma and the Sea by Jaime Gamboa

Be a King: Dr. Martin Luther King Jr.'s Dream and You by Carole Boston Weatherford

Martin's Big Words by Doreen Rappaport

Native American Heroes: Inspiring Leaders by Dawn Quigley

Nibi Emosaawdang: The Water Walker by Joanne Robertson

Poetry for Young People: Langston Hughes by David Roessel

Redwoods by Jason Chin

So Tall Within: Sojourner Truth's Long Walk Toward Freedom by Gary D. Schmidt

When We Were Alone by David A. Robertson

Write to Me: Letters from Japanese American Children to the Librarian They Left Behind by Cynthia Grady

Grades 6–8

Bad Boy by Walter Dean Myers

Bluebird by Sharon Cameron

Confetti Girl by Diana López

Echo by Pam Muñoz Ryan

Inside Out and Back Again by Thanhha Lai

The Life I'm In by Sharon Flake

Martin Rising: Requiem for a King by Andrea Davis Pinkney

One Crazy Summer by Rita Williams-Garcia

Where the Mountain Meets the Moon by Grace Lin

Where We Go From Here by Lucas Rocha

Professional References Cited

ACT (2014). The condition of college & career readiness 2013: Hispanic students. Retrieved from http://www.act.org/newsroom/data/2013/states/hispanic.html

Agar, M. (1994). *Language shock: Understanding the culture of conversation*. New York: Morrow.

Alameddine, M. M., & Ahwal, H. W. (2016), Inquiry based teaching in literature classrooms. *Procedia—Social and Behavioral Sciences* (October 14, 2016).

Allington, R. L., & Gabriel, R. E. (2012, March). Every child, every day. *Educational Leadership*. The Association of Supervision and Curriculum Development (ASCD), *69*(6).

Allington, R. L., and McGill-Franzen, A. (2013). *Summer reading: Closing the rich/poor achievement gap*. New York: Teachers College Press.

Allington, R. L. (2002). What I've learned about effective reading instruction from a decade of studying exemplary elementary classroom teachers. *Phi Delta Kappan, 83*(10), 740–747.

Allington, R. L, McCuiston, K., & Billen, M. (2015). What research says about text complexity and learning to read. *The Reading Teacher, 68*(7), 491–501.

Anderson, R. C., Hiebert, E. H., Scott, J. A., & Wilkinson, I. A. G. (1985). *Becoming a nation of readers: The report of the Commission on Reading*. Washington, DC: National Institute of Education.

Anderson, R. C., Wilson, P. T., & Fielding, L. G. (1988). Growth in reading and how children spend their time outside of school. *Reading Research Quarterly, 23*(3), 285–303.

Atwell, N. (2014). *In the middle: A lifetime of learning about writing, reading, and adolescents* (3rd ed.). Portsmouth, NH: Heinemann.

Beck, I. L., & McKeown, M. G. (2001). Text talk: Capturing the benefits of read aloud experiences for young children. *The Reading Teacher* (September 2001).

Beck, I. L., & Sandora, C. A. (2016). *Illuminating comprehension and close reading*. New York: The Guilford Press.

Beers, K. (2003). *When kids can't read: What teachers can do*. Portsmouth, NH: Heinemann.

Beers, K., & Probst, R. (2020). *Forged by reading: The power of a literate life*. New York: Scholastic.

Bergin, C., & Bergin, D. (2009). Attachment in the classroom. *Educational Psychology Review, 21*, 141–170.

Bishop, R. S. (1990). Mirrors, window, and sliding glass doors. *Perspectives, 6*(3), ix-xi.

Blachowicz, C., & Fisher, P. (2015). Best practices in vocabulary instruction. In L. Gambrell & L. M. Morrow (Eds.), *Best practices in literacy instruction* (5th ed.) (pp. 195–222). New York: Guilford Press.

Brackett, M. A. (2018). The emotional intelligence we owe students and educators. *ASCD* (October 1, 2018).

Braxton, B. (2007). Developing your reading-aloud skills. *Teacher Librarian, 34*(4), 56–57, 68.

California Department of Education. (2015). *English language arts/English language development framework for California public schools: Kindergarten through grade twelve*. Sacramento, CA: California Department of Education.

Cazden, C. (1988). *Classroom discourse: The language of teaching and learning*. Portsmouth, NH: Heinemann.

Center on the Developing Child at Harvard University. (2015). *Supportive relationships and active skill-building strengthen the foundations of resilience: Working paper 13*. Retrieved from www.developingchild.harvard.edu

Cosier, S. (2021). Listening to a story helps hospitalized kids heal. *Scientific American* (October 1, 2021).

Culham, R. (2010). *Traits of writing: The complete guide for middle school*. New York: Scholastic.

Cullinan, B. E. (2000). Independent reading and school achievement. *School Library Media Research, 3*,1–23.

Cunningham, A. E., & Stanovich, K. E. (1998, Spring/Summer). What reading does for the mind. *American Educator*, 8–17.

Cunningham, A. E., & Zibulsky, J. (2014). *Book smart: How to develop and support successful, motivated readers*. Oxford, England: Oxford University Press.

Currie, L. (2014, October 17). Why teaching kindness in schools is essential to reduce bullying. [Blog post]. Retrieved from http://www.edutopia.org/blog/teaching-kindness-essential-reduce-bullying-lisa-currie

DeCasper, A. J., & Spence, M. (1986). Prenatal maternal speech influences newborns' perception of speech sounds. *Infant Behavior and Development, 9*(2), 133–150.

Diener, E., & Seligman, M. E. P. (2002). Very happy people. *Psychological Science, 13*, 80–83.

Djikic, M., Oatley, K., & Moldoveanu, M. (2013). Reading other minds: Effects of literature on empathy. *Scientific Study of Literature, 3*(1), 28–47.

Duke, N. (2014). *Inside information: Developing powerful readers and writers through project-based instruction*. New York: Scholastic.

Duke, N., & Martin, N. (2015). Best practices in informational text comprehension instruction. In L. Gambrell & L. M. Morrow (Eds.), *Best practices in literacy instruction* (5th ed.) (pp. 249–267). New York: Guilford Press.

Dyson, A. H. (1995). The courage to write: Child meaning making in a contested world. *Language Arts, 72*(5), 324–333.

Eccles, J. S., & Wigfield, A. (2002). Motivational beliefs, values, and goals. *Annual Review of Psychology, 53*, 109–132.

Edmundson, M. (2015). *Self and soul: A defense of ideals.* Cambridge, MA: Harvard University Press.

Education Week. (2012, June 7). Diplomas Count 2012: Trailing behind, moving forward: Latino students in U.S. schools. Retrieved from http://www.edweek.org/ew/toc/2012/06/07/

Engel, S. (2015). *The hungry mind: The origins of curiosity in childhood.* Cambridge, MA: Harvard University Press.

Espinoza, C. M., & Ascenzi-Moreno, L. (2021). *Rooted in strength: Using translanguaging to grow multilingual readers and writers.* New York: Scholastic.

Evans, M., Kelley, J., Sikorac, J., & Treimand, D. (2010). Family scholarly culture and educational success: books and schooling in 27 nations. *Research in Social Stratification and Mobility, 28*, 171–197.

Fisher, D., Flood, J., Lapp, D., & Frey, N. (2004). Interactive read alouds: Is there a common set of implementation practices? *The Reading Teacher, 58*, 8–17.

Freire, P. (1970). *Pedagogy of the oppressed.* New York: Continuum.

Gallup. (2014). *Postsecondary education aspirations and barriers.* Washington, DC: Gallup Inc.

Gates, B. (2000). *Business @ the speed of thought: Succeeding in the digital economy.* New York: Penguin.

Ginwright, S. (2015). *Hope and healing in urban education: How urban activists and teachers are reclaiming matters of the heart.* New York: Routledge.

Goleman, D. (2011). *Leadership: The power of emotional intelligence.* Florence, MA: More Than Sound.

Graham, S., & Hebert, M. (2010). Writing to read: A meta-analysis of the impact of writing and writing instruction on reading. *Harvard Educational Review, 81*(4).

Graham, S., & Perin, D. (2007). *Writing next: Effective strategies to improve writing of adolescents in middle and high schools: A report to the Carnegie Corporation of New York.* Washington, DC: Alliance for Excellent Education.

Guthrie, J. (2004). Teaching for literacy engagement. *Journal of Literacy Research, 36*(1), 1–30.

Guthrie, J. T., & Greaney, V. (1991). Literacy acts. In R. Barr, M. L. Kamil, P. Mosenthal, & P. D. Pearson (Eds.), *Handbook of reading research, Vol. II* (pp. 68–96). New York: Longman.

Harvard Business Review. (2014, August 27). Curiosity is as important as intelligence. Retrieved from https://hbr.org/2014/08/curiosity-is-as-important-as-intelligence/

Heard, G. (2016). *Heart maps: Helping students create and craft authentic writing.* Portsmouth, NH: Heinemann.

Hiebert, E. H., & Reutzel, D. R. (Eds.). (2010). *Revisiting silent reading: New directions for teachers and researchers.* Newark, DE: International Reading Association.

Hutton, J. S., Horowitz-Kraus, T., Mendelsohn, A. L., DeWitt, T., & Holland, S. K. (2015). Home reading environment and brain activation in preschool children listening to stories. *Pediatrics, 136*(3), 466–478.

Johnson, D., & Blair, A. (2003). The importance and use of student self-selected literature to reading engagement in an elementary reading curriculum. *Reading Horizons, 43*(3), 181–202.

Kalb, G., & van Ours, J. C. (2013). *Reading to young children: A head-start in life?* Melbourne, Australia: The Melbourne Institute of Applied Economic and Social Research. Working Paper No. 17/13. Retrieved from https://www.melbourneinstitute.com/downloads/working_paper_series/wp2013n17.pdf

Kidd, D. C., and Castano, E. (2013). Reading literary fiction improves theory of mind. *Science, 342*(6156), 377–380.

Krashen, S. D. (2004). *The power of reading: Insights From the research.* Santa Barbara, CA: Libraries Unlimited.

Laminack, L. L. (2019). *The ultimate read-alound resource, 2nd edition.* New York: Scholastic.

Lesesne, T. S. (2006). Reading aloud: A worthwhile investment? *Voices From the Middle, 13*(4), 50–54.

Lewis, C. (2001). *Literary practices as social acts: Power, status, and cultural norms in the classroom.* Mahwah, NJ: Lawrence Erlbaum Associates, Inc.

Litwin, E., & Pepin, G.(2020). *The power of joyful reading: Help your young readers soar to success!* New York: Scholastic.

Miller, D. (2009). *The book whisperer: Awakening the inner reader in every child.* San Francisco, CA: Jossey-Bass.

Moje, E. B., Overby, M., Tysvaer, N., & Morris, K. (2008). The complex world of adolescent literacy: Myths, motivations, and mysteries. *Harvard Educational Review, 78*(1), 107–154.

Muhammad, G. (2020). *Cultivating genius: An equity framework for culturally and historically responsive literacy.* New York: Scholastic.

National Scientific Council on the Developing Child. (2015). Supportive relationships and active skill-building strengthen the foundations of resilience: working paper 13. Retrieved from http://developingchild.harvard.edu/resources/supportive-relationships-and-active-skill-building-strengthen-the-foundations-of-resilience/

Noddings, N. (2003). *Happiness and education.* Cambridge, UK: Cambridge University Press.

O'Grady, P. (2012, October 26). Positive psychology in the classroom. friendship: The key to happiness. [Blog post]. Retrieved from https://www.psychologytoday.com/blog/positive-psychology-in-the-classroom/201210/friendship-the-key-happiness

Paul, A. M. (2012, March). *Your brain on fiction.* Retrieved from http://www.nytimes.com/2012/03/18/opinion/sunday/the-neuroscience-of-your-brain-on-fiction.html?_r=0

Pelkey, L. (2013). In the LD Bubble. In M. Adams, W. Blumenfeld, C. Castaneda, H. Hackman, M. Peters, & and X. Zuniga (Eds.), (3rd ed.) *Reading for Diversity and Social Justice.* New York: Routledge.

Reardon, S. F. (2011). The widening academic achievement gap between the rich and the poor: New evidence and possible explanations. In G. J. Duncan & R. J. Murnane, (Eds.), *Whither opportunity? Rising inequality, schools, and children's life chances* (91–117). New York: The Russell Sage Foundation.

Rittner, C., & Myers, S. (Eds.) (1989). *The courage to care.* New York: NYU Press.

Rowe, D., Fain, J. G., & Fink, L. (2013). The family backpack project: Responding to dual-language texts through family journals. *Language Arts, 90*(6), 402–416.

Rumberger, R. (2011). *Dropping out: Why kids drop out of high school and what can be done about it.* Cambridge, MA: Harvard University Press.

Schaps, E. (March/April 2009). Creating caring school communities. *Leadership,* 8–11.

Scharer, P. L. (2018). *Responsive literacy: A comprehensive framework.* New York: Scholastic.

Schneider, L. (2020). *Empathy is the highest level of critical thinking.* NCTE Blog (October 1, 2020).

Scholastic Inc. (2016). *Kids & Family Reading Report, Fifth Edition.* New York: Scholastic.

Selman, R. (2007). *The promotion of social awareness: Powerful lessons from the partnership of developmental theory and classroom practice.* New York: Russell Sage Foundation.

Smith, F. (1987). *Joining the literacy club: Further essays into education.* Portsmouth, NH: Heinemann.

Sobol, T. (2013). *My life in school.* Scarsdale, NY: Public Schools of Tomorrow.

Sotomayor, S. *Fresh Air. An interview with Terry Gross.* National Public Radio: January 13, 2014. Web Aug. 30 2015.

Sparks, S.D. (2021). The SEL skills that may matter most for academic success: Curiosity and persistence. *Education Week* (October 29, 2021).

Stetser, M., & Stillwell, R. (2014). *Public high school four-year on-time graduation rates and event dropout rates: School years 2010–11 and 2011–12: First Look* (NCES 2014-391). U.S. Department of Education. Washington, DC: National Center for Education Statistics. Retrieved [date] from http://nces.ed.gov/pubsearch

Sullivan, A., & Brown, M. (2013). *Social inequalities in cognitive scores at age 16: The role of reading.* London, UK: Centre for Longitudinal Studies.

Taylor, B. M., Frye, B. J., & Maruyama, G. M. (1990). Time spent reading and reading growth. *American Educational Research Journal, 27*(2), 351–362.

Trelease, J. (2006). *The Read-Aloud Handbook.* New York: Penguin Group.

UNESCO Institute for Statistics (2013). *Adult and youth literacy: National, regional and global trends, 1985-2015.* Montreal, Quebec: UNESCO Institute for Statistics.

U.S. Bureau of Labor Statistics. (2021). Employment status of the civilian population 25 years and older by educational attainment. https://www.bls.gov/news.release/empsit.t04.htm

Vezzali, L., Stathi, S., Giovannini, D., Capozza, D., & Trifiletti, E. (2014). The greatest Harry Potter magic of all: Reducing prejudice. *Journal of Applied Social Psychology, 45*(2), 105–121.

Wiley, T. G., & de Klerk, G. (2010). Common myths and stereotypes regarding literacy and language diversity in the multilingual United States. In M. Farr, L. Seloni, & J. Song (Eds.), *Ethnolinguistic diversity and education: Language, literacy, and culture* (pp. 23–43). New York: Routledge.

Wilhelm, J. (1996). *You gotta BE the book: Teaching engaged and reflective reading with adolescents.* New York: Teachers College Press.

Index

7 Strengths Framework, 7–12, 28–41
  charts of, 36,146, 199
  actions and routines
    for Belonging, 49, 52, 54, 55
    for Friendship, 63, 66, 67, 68
    for Kindness, 75, 78, 80, 81
    for Curiosity, 89, 92, 94, 95
    for Confidence, 103, 106, 107
    for Courage, 115, 118, 119, 120
    for Hope, 127, 130, 131, 132
  and collaborating with peers, 145
  and conferring, 157
  and goals for independent reading, 155
  and identity building, 147
  and mentor texts, 151
  and partnering, 144
  and read-alouds, 138
  and reading celebrations, 148
  and small-group instruction, 141
  and text investigations, 140–141
  during first 21 days, 189–190

A
academic achievement, through super reading, 15
access, importance of, 152–154
access to texts, as fundamental for super reading, 24, 39–40
achievement, high, through super reading, 17–18
active listening, 99–100, 157–158
asking questions vs. correct answers, 86
aspirations, educational, studies about, 97–98
assessment tools, 170–186
asynchronous instruction, 167
authentic communication, as fundamental for super reading, 23
author study, 40, 87, 89
author's craft, 16, 57
  in text investigations, 139
awareness building, 147

B
"being" to "becoming," from, courage in, 109–110
Belonging, 10, 32–33, 42–55
  children's texts for, 200
  conferring checklist for, 184
  during first 21 days, 189
  goal-setting tool for, 180
  questions to elicit stories about, 37
bilinguals, 22, 57, 137, 159–160
biographies, to promote courage, 112
book baskets, 49, 54, 86, 94
book chats, virtual, 67
book club, 59, 68, 89, 137, 151
book exchange, 61
book talk, 47
bookmark buddies, 63

book-matching, 153
Books for Boys initiative, 109
brain scans of fictional vs. real-life experiences, 18–19
breakthroughs, practice needed for, 99
bullying, 34

C
celebrations, reading, 148, 159
checklists
  for digital citizenship, 170, 173
  7 Strengths conferring, 171, 184-185
  7 Strengths partnership, 194
choice, book, 24–25, 39, 139, 152–154
citing evidence, phrases to scaffold, 140
civic engagement, 15
classroom library, 149–150
  curation of, 24, 111, 123
  personalized, 45–46
classroom management, 161–169
cognitive functions, 18–19, 136
collaboration, 60–61, 100, 142–145, 148
  Super Reader Rubrics for, 178
comic books, 16, 24, 38, 39, 99, 123, 151
communication, centrality of, 17
community membership, 26, 32–33, 48–49, 61, 78, 178
comprehension, Super Reader Rubrics for, 177
conferring, 157
  7 Strengths Checklist, 171, 184-185
Confidence, 10–11, 15, 34, 96–107
  children's texts for, 202
  conferring checklist for, 185
  during first 21 days, 190
  goal-setting tool for, 182
  questions to elicit stories about, 37
conversations about books, 47, 99, 100, 157
  stems to scaffold, 143
Courage, 10, 35–36, 108–120
  children's texts for, 202–203
  conferring checklist for, 185
  during first 21 days, 190
  goal-setting tool for, 182
  questions to elicit stories about, 37
  types of, 111
Curiosity, 10, 34, 82–95
  children's texts for, 201–202
  conferring checklist for, 184
  during first 21 days, 189–190
  goal-setting tool for, 181
  questions to elicit stories about, 37

D
digital citizenship, 81
  7 Strengths Checklist for, 170, 173
digital materials, 9, 24, 39, 92
digital spaces, 45, 52, 67
digital technologies, 14, 20–21, ,67, 106, 167

disengaged student vs. hopeful student, 130
diverse texts, 30–32, 153
  in classroom library, 45–46
dreaming, 37, 125, 190
dual-language learner, 22, 57, 137, 159–160

E
emergent readers, and read-alouds, 136–137
emotional intelligence, 72
empathy, 18–19, 59, 66, 72, 123
engagement, 24–25, 34, 145–146, 148, 161–162, 168–169
  Super Reader Rubrics for, 176
environments, supportive, 26, 46–47, 145–151
equity, 31

F
failure, as positive step, 100, 120
family involvement, 39, 45
  for Belonging, 53–55
  for Friendship, 66–68
  for Kindness, 78–81
  for Curiosity, 92–95
  for Confidence, 106–107
  for Courage, 118–120
  for Hope, 130–132
fictional experiences, empathy and, 18–19
First 21 Days, The, (planning tool), 189–190
fluency, Super Reader Rubrics for, 177
  stamina, Super Reader Rubrics for, 177
Focus Lessons
  on Belonging, 48–49
  on Friendship, 62–63
  on Kindness, 74–75
  on Curiosity, 88–89
  on Confidence, 101–103
  on Courage, 114–115
  on Hope, 126–127
Friendship, 10, 33, 56–68
  actions for, 63, 66, 68
  children's texts for, 200–201
  conferring checklist for, 184
  during first 21 days, 189
  goal-setting tool for, 180
  in brief, 33
friendship development, five stages of, 58–59

G
goal setting, 32, 124, 155, 157
  assessment tools for, 171
  checklists for, 180–183
  planning tools for, 194
  rubrics for, 179
graphic novels, 24, 99

H

health, friendship and, 58–59
heart maps, 44–45, 49, 54, 126–127, 189, 190
heroes, as role models, 98–99, 112–113
home language, 16, 31, 57, 81, 137
home, reading at, 39. *See also* family involvement
Hope, 10, 36, 121–132
   as basic human need, 122–123
   children's texts for, 203
   conferring checklist for, 185
   during first 21 days, 190
   goal-setting tool for, 183
   questions to elicit stories about, 37

I

independent reading, structured, 26, 152–160
   instruction during, 153–157
information age, 20
inhibitors of learning, 70–71
inquiry-based instruction, 85
instructional read-aloud, 136
Interactive Reading Lessons, 21
   on Belonging, 50–51
   on Friendship, 64–65
   on Kindness, 76–77
   on Curiosity, 90–91
   on Confidence, 104–105
   on Courage, 116–117
   on Hope, 128–129
"interestingness" of a text, 24–25
Internet, use of, 29, 66, 92

K

Kindness, 10, 33–34, 69–81
   children's texts for, 201
   conferring checklist for, 184
   during first 21 days, 189
   goal-setting tool for, 181
   questions to elicit stories about, 37

L

listening attentively, 60, 99–100, 157
LitCamp, 7, 10, 29, 70, 73, 97, 151
   schedule for (planning tool), 195
literacy development, research about, 136–137
"literate environment", 24–25
literature, power of, 36, 59–60, 85–86, 98–99
LitWorld, 19, 30, 44, 124, 138
Log, Super Reader, (assessment tool), 171, 186
lower-level texts, value of, 158, 160

M

management strategies, classroom, 161–169
mental health, friendship and, 33
mentor texts, 150–151
minutes for daily independent reading, minimum, 154
modalities of reading, 9, 14, 20–21, 39–40, 147
   access to diverse, 31, 39–40

motivation, and confidence, 97–98

N

noise level, strategies to control, 162–163
norms, classroom, establishing, during first 21 days, 189

O

obedience vs. active inquiry, 83

P

pandemic, effects of, 8, 28–29
participatory education, 12
partnering, 60, 142–144, 164
   7 Strengths checklist for, 189–190
   for emerging bilinguals, 159
peer conversation, 47
peer-to-peer instruction, 86–87
performance-based work, 100
perspectives, 59, 71–72, 87
planning tools, 187–197
pleasure in reading, super reader's, 27, 38–39
poem, as world-changing, 121–122
point of view, 59, 71–72, 87
positive experiences, 70–71
practice, 21, 39–40, 99, 154
principles, fundamental, of super readers, 21–27
project-based learning, 34, 69, 142

Q

questioning, modeled, 87
quiet voices, during first 21 days, 190

R

read-alouds, 22, 39, 46–47, 72, 123, 135–138
reading, 9–12, 20–21, 78, 144–145, 148
   modeling, 25, 41
   safe environment for, 38
   and super reading, 21, 25, 26
   made "visible," 138–139
   and writing process, 22–23
reading interactively, 21, 25
reading partners, 142–144
"reading the word," 20, 30
rereading, 24, 40, 162
   for emerging bilinguals, 159–160
resilience, emotional, 19–20, 70
risk taking, 97
ritual read-aloud, 136–138
role models, kindness as act of, 74–75
round-robin reading, vs. read-aloud, 137
routines, 168
   for Belonging, 55
   for Friendship, 68
   for Kindness, 81
   for Curiosity, 95
   for Confidence, 107
   for Courage, 120
   for Hope, 132
rubrics, 170, 174–179

S

sense of self, through super reading, 19–20
sharing thinking, phrases to scaffold, 139
shy children, 61, 100, 145

skills, taught during structured independent reading, 155–156
small-group instruction, 141–142
social justice, kindness as act of, 70
social well-being, through super reading, 15
speaking/listening, to promote confidence, 99–100, 106
stamina, 10, 98, 148, 156, 159, 190
storytelling, 22
strategies, reading, 25
   during first 21 days, 190
   for striving readers, 158–159
   taught during structured independent reading, 155–156
striving readers, supporting, 158–159
success, tied to confidence, 99–100
   as rules-based game, 134
   top 10 ways for nurturing, 37–41
superhero profiles, to promote confidence, 101–103

T

talking about books, 40, 47
teacher-student relationship, 43
technology use, 118, 130, 166–167, 168, 190
tenderness, valuing, 71–72
text investigations, 138–141
text types for classroom library (chart), 149
time, daily, for reading, 39–40, 146, 154
tough spots, characters in, 98
translanguaging, 21, 31

U

understanding, through super reading, 18–19

V

variety of texts, 153
virtual spaces, 45, 52, 67
visuals, for emerging bilinguals, 159
voluminous reading, benefits of, 17, 23, 148
volunteering, to promote kindness, 78
vulnerability, and courage, 35

W

"Welcome to My World" board, 46, 49, 189
well-being, friendship and, 58–59
what, how, and *why* we read, modeled, 138–139
whole-small-whole teaching sequence, 135
mirrors, windows, and sliding glass doors, 30
World Read Aloud Day, 73, 138
writing, 22–23, 31, 75, 146, 163,
   bilingual students and, 159–160
   with mentor texts, 150
   about reading, 34, 44–45, 57, 158–159
   as thinking, 160